BILLY GRAHAM

Evangelistic Association

Always Good News.

Dear Friend,

I am pleased to send you this copy of excerpts from *What Every Christian Ought to Know* by the late Adrian Rogers, a three-term president of the Southern Baptist Convention. Dr. Rogers was a friend of my father and spoke often at the Billy Graham Training Center at The Cove.

In the passages we have collected for this edition, Dr. Rogers provides a basic and straightforward explanation of many Christian doctrines. At a time when our beliefs and values are under attack from the culture at large, it is important for believers to know what we believe and be able to explain it to others. Whether you are a brand-new Christian or have been following Christ for years, I pray that these selections will lead you to *"move beyond the elementary teachings about Christ and be taken forward to maturity"* (Hebrews 6:1, NIV).

For more than 60 years, the Billy Graham Evangelistic Association has worked to take the Good News of Jesus Christ throughout the world by every effective means available, and I'm excited about what God will do in the years ahead.

We would appreciate knowing how our ministry has touched your life. May God richly bless you.

Sincerely,

Franklin Graham
President

If you would like to know more about our ministry, please contact us:

IN THE U.S.:

Billy Graham Evangelistic Association
1 Billy Graham Parkway
Charlotte, NC 28201-0001
BillyGraham.org
info@bgea.org
Toll-free: 1-877-247-2426

IN CANADA:

Billy Graham Evangelistic
   Association of Canada
20 Hopewell Way NE
Calgary, AB T3J 5H5
BillyGraham.ca
Toll-free: 1-888-393-0003

WHAT EVERY CHRISTIAN OUGHT TO KNOW

ADRIAN ROGERS
with STEVE ROGERS

This *Billy Graham Library Selection* is published with
permission from the B&H Publishing Group.

B&H
PUBLISHING GROUP
Nashville, Tennessee

A *Billy Graham Library Selection* designates materials that are appropriate for a well-rounded collection of quality Christian literature, including both classic and contemporary reading and reference materials.

This *Billy Graham Library Selection* is published by the Billy Graham Evangelistic Association with permission from B&H Publishing Group.

Copyright ©2005, 2012
by Adrian Rogers
All rights reserved
Printed in the United States of America

ISBN: 978-1-59328-395-7
Previous ISBN: 978-1-4336-7785-4

Published by B&H Publishing Group
Nashville, Tennessee

Dewey Decimal Classification: 230
Subject Heading: CHRISTIAN DOCTRINE

Unless otherwise noted Scripture quotations are from the New King James Version, copyright ©1979, 1980, 1982, Thomas Nelson, Inc., Publishers. Scripture quotations marked KJV are from the King James Version. Scripture quotations marked NASB are from the New American Standard Bible, ©The Lockman Foundation, 1960, 1962, 1963, 1968, 1971, 1972, 1973, 1975, 1977; used by permission.

Contents

Preface   What You Don't Know *Can* Hurt You   1

Chapter 1   Every Christian Ought to Know
the Bible Is the Word of God   5

Chapter 2   Every Christian Ought to Know
the Assurance of Salvation   27

Chapter 3   Every Christian Ought to Know
about Eternal Security   51

Chapter 4   Every Christian Ought to Know
How to Pray (with Power)   73

Chapter 5   Every Christian Ought to Know
How to Understand the Bible   93

Epilogue   It's Not How Much You Know,
It's How Much You *Grow*   111

Preface

What You Don't Know
Can Hurt You

Wiped Out!

The waves were enormous, much bigger than those in my native state of Florida. We were in Maui, Hawaii, and I was excited. I love to bodysurf. Catch a wave just right, and you can ride without a board all the way to the beach.

I worked my way out to where the waves were breaking. I saw my wave building up. This would be a great ride. I knew I had to catch it just right. At the special moment I put my head down and gave a kick. The action really began.

The monster wave didn't take me to the beach. It picked me up like a rag doll and "body slammed" me on the ocean floor. The lights went out. I was numb. "Let me check. Can I move my legs, my arms?" Nothing was broken. I made my way carefully to the shore.

When I got back on solid ground, I turned to see the big sign posted:

NO BODYSURFING.
Serious Spinal Injury May Result.

There was the warning in plain sight, but I was saturated with ignorance. So much for the old proverb, *What you don't know can't hurt you.*

Education is costly, but ignorance may be devastating. There are some basic truths that every Christian ought to know. Many founder in a sea of moral relativism and vague religious opinions. Some may be body slammed, like I was, because they do not know.

Our society boasts about pluralism (there is room for every idea) but really practices syncretism by blending all religious thought into a bland mixture of spiritual pablum. Americans love to prate about values but are quickly intimidated when the question is asked, "Whose values?" It is more morality by majority than biblical virtues.

Some speak of education as the answer to most everything, and yet the more we know, the deeper we sink. We are "always learning and never able to come to the knowledge of the truth" (2 Tim. 3:7). Our generation has substituted facts for truth. We don't ask, "Is it true?" We just want to know, "Does it work?" Many Christians don't grow because they don't know. Facts are like a recipe, but truth is like a meal. Digest a truth and it will change your life.

"Buy the truth, and do not sell it" (Prov. 23:23).

- We must *prize* the truth.
  There is no way to be a happy, victorious Christian without a firm conviction based on foundational truth.

- We must *purchase* the truth.

  "Buy the truth." Salvation is free, but the quest for truth is costly. Yet while discipleship is costly, ignorance is far more costly. The quest for truth will cost precious time, discipline, and obedience, but it is worth it.

- We must *preserve* the truth.

  "Do not sell it." Some will tempt us to "sell out." Don't do it. Get a bulldog grip on the truth and never let go.

> *When the child of God*
> *Loves the Word of God*
> *And sees the Son of God,*
> *He is changed by the Spirit of God*
> *Into the image of God*
> *For the glory of God*
> *Because he has found the truth of God.*

This book deals with the fundamental truth that *Every Christian Ought to Know.* It is written to be clear but not simplistic. It is for the new believer but also for those who seem bogged down in their Christian walk.

1

Every Christian Ought to Know
the Bible Is the Word of God

---

*All Scripture is given by inspiration of God,
and is profitable for doctrine, for reproof, for correction, for
instruction in righteousness, that the man of God may be
complete, thoroughly equipped for every good work.*

2 TIMOTHY 3:16–17

The starting place in Christian growth is to have a firm conviction about the inspiration and authority of the Bible. In this chapter I want to give some solid reasons to have this assurance. Believe me when I tell you this is the starting place. You will not make solid progress without it.

Man Has Only Three Problems

While on an airplane, I was browsing the magazine selection looking for a newspaper. I met a man there who asked what kind of newspaper I was looking for. I responded frankly that I was looking for a conservative newspaper.

He looked me up and down and said, "I'm looking for a liberal newspaper." He was wearing a dark pin-striped suit, and I asked him what he did. He responded that he was a lawyer and in return asked me what I did. I told him I was a Baptist preacher.

He was interested in what I read, and I told him that I read books, journals, and newspapers, but that I primarily read the Bible.

"You don't read any wider than that?" he asked.

"No, not really."

"Do you speak to people?"

"All the time."

He said, "Well then, how do you know what people's needs and what their problems are if you don't read any more widely than that?"

I said to this lawyer, "Man has only three problems: sin, sorrow, and death."

He said, "No, there are more problems than that."

I said, "All right, think about it and tell me a fourth problem."

He thought for a while, and then he said, "Man has only three problems."

Every other problem in the world is indeed just a subset of sin, sorrow, death, and the Bible is the *only book on earth* that has the answer to all three conditions. For this reason it is important that you understand and have a rock-ribbed assurance that the Bible is the Word of God. It is not the Book of the Month; it is the Book of the Ages.

There Is a War on the Bible

The devil hates this book and would like to destroy it. Some despise the Bible; others just deny it; still others distort it and have warped, misused, and abused it. But I believe the greatest enemy of the Bible is the so-called Christian who simply ignores the Bible or disregards it. He gives only lip service to it.

> *"These hath God married and no man shall part:*
> *Dust in the Bible and drought in the heart."*

I have been serving Jesus for a long time, and the thing that keeps me going is truth and conviction. This conviction is not based on my feelings but on what I know is truth. Feelings come and go, but God's Word never wavers.

Why is this so important?

- Your salvation depends on understanding the gospel message of the Bible.
- Your assurance depends on resting in the truth of the Bible.
- Your spiritual growth depends on living by the principles of the Bible.
- Your power in witness depends on the confidence you have in the Word of God.

Therefore, you must be absolutely certain that the Bible is the Word of God. I want to give you some principles that have confirmed this certainty for me. Let me say that beyond these objective arguments, there is the sweet affirmation of the Holy Spirit to my heart concerning the Word of God. Jesus said, "My sheep hear My voice" (John 10:27). Think with me about the following confirmations of the inspiration of the Bible.

The Bible Is Shown to Be the Word of God Because of Its Scientific Accuracy

Scientific accuracy confirms the Bible is the Word of God. This first concept is the same one most often used to dispute the validity of the Bible by those who deny it. It is commonly assumed that, of course, there must be scientific errors in the Bible. Before you say that, however, make certain you know two things: *science* and *the Bible.* Most often those who claim scientific errors in the Bible do not clearly understand either subject. And those who do understand science must admit that it is in a continual state of flux, constantly changing. The accepted science of yesterday is not necessarily the science of today. It has been estimated that the library in the Louvre in Paris has three and a half miles of books on science. Most every one of them is obsolete.[1]

In 1861 the French Academy of Science wrote a pamphlet stating there were fifty-one incontrovertible scientific facts that proved the Bible not true. Today there is not a reputable scientist on Earth that believes one of those fifty-one so-called facts.[2] The point is, science is changing. God's Word does not change! Let me give a few examples:

The Earth Is Suspended in Space

One of the most fundamental scientific facts that you and I agree is true today is that our Earth is suspended in space. Ancient cultures did not always know this. The ancient Egyptians used to believe the Earth was supported by pillars. The Greeks believed the world was carried on the back of a giant whose name was Atlas. And the Hindus believed something even more ridiculous—that the Earth was resting on the backs of gigantic elephants. Then somebody said, "But wait a minute, what are the elephants standing on?" The answer was, "The elephants are standing on the back of a huge tortoise—a giant turtle." Then somebody asked, "What is the turtle resting on?" The answer, "Well, that turtle is on the back of a huge coiled serpent." And somebody said, "What is the serpent on?" The conclusion was that the serpent was swimming in a great cosmic sea. This was the science of that day!

When you and I pick up the Word of God, we do not find any such mythology. Job spoke of the Lord in chapter 26 verse 7: "He stretches out the north over the *empty* space; he hangs *the earth on nothing.*" Job is perhaps the oldest piece of literature known to man. How did Job know the Earth is suspended in space? Job could only know through divine inspiration. The Bible says in 2 Timothy 3:16 that "all Scripture is given by inspiration of God."

The Earth Is Round, Not Flat

We also take for granted that the Earth is round. Do we know this by natural observation? Not at all. You've seen pictures from outer space, and perhaps you have traveled around the world, so you take it for granted. But people didn't always know that the Earth was round. Remember that little saying from when you were in school, "In 1492, Columbus sailed the ocean blue"? They warned, "Columbus, you had better be careful; you might sail off the edge of the Earth."

Even as late as 1492, people did not know that the Earth is round. Yet Isaiah, in 750 BC, said, "It is He [God] who sits above the circle of the earth" (Isa. 40:22). The word for *circle* in the Hebrew is *chuwg,* which means "globe or sphere."[3]

How did Job know that God hung the Earth upon nothing? How did Isaiah know 750 years before Christ that the Earth is round? "Holy men of God spoke as they were moved by the Holy Spirit" (2 Pet. 1:21).

The Bible teaches that when Jesus comes again, it will be both daylight and dark. For example, "There will be two men in one bed: the one will be taken and the other will be left. Two men will be in the field; the one will be taken and the other left" (Luke 17:34–36). That seems contradictory. But while it will be light on one side of the globe, it will be dark on the other side when Jesus Christ comes again. Of course, all of this did not take the one who created the world by surprise; He knew all of it.

The Stars Cannot Be Counted

Here is another scientific fact relating to the science of the Bible. The stars in our galaxy are beyond ability to number. You and I would never be so foolish as to try to count the stars. But there was one man who laid down his pen, rubbed his eyes, and was weary because he had counted the stars, or so he thought. He was an astronomer 150 years before Christ. This man's name was Hipparchus, and he was the astronomer and scientist of his day. His study yielded 1,022 stars. He had counted the stars, he had made his chart—1,022 stars—and that was science.

His findings were considered accurate for 250 years, and then along came Ptolemy who began to count the stars and said, "Did Hipparchus say there are 1,022 stars? How absurd—there are 1,056 stars." His count had upgraded the science of the day for a while.

About thirteen hundred years later, a young medical student named Galileo invented his first crude telescope, turned it up to the heavens, and looked beyond those stars that could be seen with the naked eye. There were more stars—and more stars—and hundreds and thousands and millions and billions and hundreds of billions of stars on and on and on! No fool would ever dare try to count the stars.

A while back I was reading in a scientific journal that scientists were trying to help us to understand the size of our universe. The journal stated that there are more suns like our sun in the known universe than there are grains of sand on all the seashores of the Earth.

I'm from West Palm Beach, Florida, and I can't even imagine counting the grains of sand just in a city block! And there are more suns in our universe than there are grains of sand on all of the seashores of the Earth! Think again of Hipparchus—one, two, three—1,022 stars! He could have saved some time had he turned to the Word of God. Jeremiah 33:22 states, "The host of heaven cannot be numbered."

Job says the Earth is floating in space. Isaiah says it is a globe. Jeremiah says you can't count the number of the stars.

The Blood Circulates through the Body

Let's move away from the area of astronomy and think about human anatomy and physiology. You and I take for granted that our blood is flowing in our body and is, what some have called, "a red river of life." It was not, however, until the year 1628 that William Harvey, a medical doctor, discovered that the blood circulates throughout the body.

In college I took a course in human anatomy and physiology, and I learned all of the things the blood does. It carries fuel to the cells, carries oxygen to burn that fuel, carries away waste, fights disease, and maintains a constant temperature in the body. This is only recent knowledge, though. In the "olden days" when someone got sick, the comment would often be made, "He has bad blood." People thought they needed to get rid of some of that bad blood, so they would bleed these people. Can you imagine taking a person who is sick and draining his blood?

A barber pole looks like a piece of peppermint candy but was meant to represent a bandage. Often they would take sick people to the barber who would bleed them in order to make them well. Sometimes they would put leeches on them to take the blood out of them.

A little known fact is how George Washington, the father of our country, died. He was sick so the physicians bled him. When he didn't get well, they bled him again. He didn't get well, so they bled him a third time. They bled him to death! Could it be that ever since that time the politicians have been bleeding us to death to get even? Hmmm!

Today they might have given him a blood transfusion. The Bible tells us in Leviticus 17:14: "For it [blood] is the life of all flesh. Its blood sustains its life." The blood is the life of all flesh. How did Moses know of the life-giving property of the blood? Well, "all Scripture is given by inspiration of God." "Holy men of God spoke as they were moved by the Holy Spirit." The medical science in the Bible is truly wonderful.

Rattlesnake Fat and Worm's Blood

Dr. S. I. McMillen reports in his intriguing book *None of These Diseases* that archeologists have found a medical book called the Ebers Papyrus written by the Egyptians about fifteen hundred years before Christ, during the time of Moses.[4] The Egyptians were clever and skilled, yet they had some foolish ideas. Let me give you some of the medical knowledge that was in the Ebers Papyrus. I don't suggest you follow this advice.

For example, if you want to prevent your hair from turning gray, you can anoint it with the blood of a black cat that has been boiled in oil or with the fat of a rattlesnake. Or, if you want to keep your hair from falling out, take six fats, namely those of the horse, the hippopotamus, the crocodile, the cat, the snake, and the ibex. And if you want to strengthen your hair, anoint it with the tooth of a donkey crushed in honey.

If you have a splinter embedded under your skin, here is the recommended medicine—worm's blood and donkey dung. Can you imagine the tetanus spores that would be in donkey dung?

Other kinds of drugs they used were lizard's blood, pig's teeth, rotten meat, moisture from pig's ears, and excreta from humans, animals, and even flies.

We are still trying to understand some of the things the Egyptians knew about embalming and a variety of other things. They were highly intelligent people. The Bible says that Moses was schooled in all the wisdom of the Egyptians. Moses went to the University of Egypt, and old Pharaoh paid his tuition. And I suppose he learned all of these things that were written in the Ebers Papyrus. Yet I am so glad that when I open the Bible, I don't find any of these absurd treatments.

Answer to the Black Plague Found in Leviticus

In Europe during the fourteenth century, there was something called "the black plague." One out of four people died from the black plague. They didn't know what to do with it. They couldn't control it. They had no concept of microbiology like we have now. Do you know what finally brought the plague to an end? The Bible! Finally they turned to Scripture. Leviticus 13:46: "All the days he has the sore [the plague] he shall be unclean. He is unclean, and he shall dwell alone; his dwelling shall be outside the camp." They learned to quarantine from the Word of God.

Although I've mentioned several areas of science where the Bible has been vindicated, I have only touched the surface of the many medical and scientific truths contained in the Bible. Frankly, I'm glad the Bible and modern science don't always agree. Science changes. The Bible—never!

The Bible Is Shown to Be the Word of God Because of Its Historical Accuracy

The Bible is not primarily a science book. It is not written to tell us how the heavens go; it is written to tell us how to go to heaven. But when it speaks on science, it is accurate. And the Bible is not primarily a book of history. It is "His story," the story of God. But you would expect to find the history of the Bible to be accurate and to be true. However, as you might suspect, the Bible has been attacked because of its history.

In the late 1800s, the scholar Dr. S. R. Driver ridiculed the idea that Moses wrote what is called the Pentateuch, the first five books of the Bible—Genesis, Exodus, Leviticus, Numbers, and Deuteronomy. Driver claimed, "In the time that Moses was supposed to have lived on the Earth, men didn't know how to write. So how could he have written the Pentateuch?"

So some scoffed at the Bible for a while until one day, in northern Egypt, a lady was spading her garden when she came across some clay tablets. They were called the Tel el-Amarna tablets and were tablets used for correspondence. They were written from people in Egypt to people in Palestine, or what we call today the Holy Land, centuries before Moses was born. Not only did they know how to write, but also they had a postal service that allowed them to send letters back and forth to one another. This proves that Moses did indeed have the capability to write the Pentateuch and also proves a learned man's opinion wrong.

In the book of Daniel is a story about the handwriting on the wall. King Belshazzar saw handwriting on the wall during a feast he made for a thousand of his lords and ladies. The gruesome handwriting told him he was weighed in the balances and found wanting. Do you remember the story? Well, scholars would laugh at that and say, "It's a fabrication. That never happened because we have the records of the ancient Babylonians, and we know that Belshazzar was not the last king of Babylon. The last king of Babylon was named Nabonitus. Obviously this would appear to be just some pious fraud, some story that somebody made up."

But one day the spade of an archeologist uncovered a cylinder, and sure enough, the name on it was Belshazzar. More records were found that showed the historians were right when they said that Nabonitus was the last king of Babylon, but they were wrong when they said that Belshazzar was not the last king of Babylon. Nabonitus and Belshazzar were father and son and had ruled together, making them both kings at the same time! Nabonitus was a big game hunter, among other things, and was often gone, leaving Belshazzar in charge. Remember what the king said to Daniel in Daniel 5:16 concerning the handwriting on the wall, "If you can read the writing and make known to me its interpretation you shall be clothed with purple and have a chain of gold around your neck, and shall be the *third* ruler in the kingdom." It makes sense now that we understand there were already two kings simultaneously.

Now what would have happened had they not found the cylinder with Belshazzar's name on it? Would the Bible be any less the Word of God? Just give people time, and maybe one day they'll catch up with the Bible. If a historian or a scientist has a good word to say about the Bible, it shouldn't give you any more faith in the Bible, just a little more faith in the scientist or the historian. The Bible has and will stand the test of time.

The Bible Is Shown to Be the Word of God Because of Its Wonderful Unity

Let me give you a third reason we can know the Bible is the Word of God. It is the wonderful unity of the Bible: one book, Genesis through Revelation, but it is also sixty-six books—thirty-nine books in the Old Testament and twenty-seven books in the New Testament. It is a compilation of books written by at least forty authors, and perhaps more. These people lived in a period of time that would span at least sixteen hundred years. They lived in about thirteen different countries and on three different continents.

Think about this. They came from all backgrounds: some were shepherds, and some were kings; some were soldiers, and others were princes; some were fishermen; some were scholars; some were historians; some were professional men, and some were common laborers. And the Bible is written in different styles and in at least three different languages. But when you bring all that together, it makes one book that has one story beginning with Genesis and going through Revelation.

- The Bible has one theme—redemption.
- The Bible has one hero—the Lord Jesus.
- The Bible has one villain—the devil.
- The Bible has one purpose—the glory of God!

All of its parts fit together. Can you imagine taking forty different people over a period of sixteen hundred years from different countries and different occupations and telling them each to write independent of one another without having read what the others had written? Put that altogether and see what kind of a hodgepodge you would have! Yet you have this wonderful unity in the Word of God.

I have been seriously studying the Bible now for many years. Throughout this study I have not found hidden faults; I have found hidden treasures and affirmations. I find an amazing interconnectedness within the Word of God. It is astounding!

Not One Stone Too Many, Not One Too Few

Dr. R. A. Torrey gave this illustration—let me paraphrase it. Suppose in your city they decided to build a monument honoring all of the fifty states in the union. Stones are gathered from each state. For example, from my home state of Florida, they get coral stone; from Georgia perhaps they would get granite; from Indiana they get limestone; from Nevada, sandstone—all of the various kinds of stones in different colors.

Then let's suppose that these stones are cut into different shapes; some are square, some are rectangular, some are cylindrical, some have a pyramid shape, some are like a trapezoid, and some have shapes that don't even have a name. They are cut out in the quarry, put in crates, and shipped by barge, by rail, and by air to your city.

Workmen uncrate these stones and begin to put them together, and they all interface, and they all interlock. There is not one stone too many, not one stone too few. No stone needs to be built up; no stone needs to be shaved down. And when they're finished, it is a magnificent temple.

You are a thinking person. Would you say that happened by chance? No, any thinking person would say that it did not happen by chance. There would have to have been a master architect who, in his mind, could see that building and had sent out the specifications to the quarry. Is that not true?

You see, when we get this Book written over a period of sixteen hundred years, forty different authors, three different languages, by men from all different walks of life and bring it together, it makes one beautiful temple of God's truth. Nothing needs to be added or taken away or embellished. There it stands— one Book! We can't say that just happened, that it was just an accident. No! The unity of the Bible is one of the wonderful proofs of the inspiration of God's Word—that all Scripture is given by inspiration of God.

The Bible Must Be the Word of God Because of Its Fulfilled Prophecy

Let me give you another reason you can believe that the Bible is the Word of God, and this is one of the great, great proofs of the inspiration of the Bible. It is the fulfilled prophecy of the Bible. This book, the Bible, has predictions of things that have yet to happen and will happen, because the Bible has predicted things that were predicted ahead of time and did happen. It has been wisely said that you can take a child of God, put him in a dungeon with a Bible and a candle and lock him away, and he will know more about what's going on in today's world with the Word of God than all the pundits in Washington. It's amazing to see history fit into the sockets of prophecy and, as you will see, actually fulfill prophecy.

We could study all kinds of fulfilled prophecy, but let's just take those related to the person and nature of Christ. Think about the Scriptures and the prophecies that were fulfilled just in the Lord Jesus Christ alone. Scholars say that Jesus fulfilled more than three hundred Old Testament prophecies. His enemies will say, "Oh sure, He fulfilled all these prophecies, but He rigged it! He just arranged that He would fulfill these prophecies." Well, if you believe that, let me tell you some of the things that He arranged.

First, He arranged to be born in Bethlehem. Could you arrange where you were going to be born? Micah 5:2 tells the prophecy that was fulfilled in Matthew 2:1–5. Then He managed for Isaiah to record details about His life seven hundred years before He was born. You can read the way Isaiah described Him in Isaiah 7, Isaiah 9, and Isaiah 53. Did you arrange to have the history of your life written before you were born?

Then He arranged to be crucified by execution on a cross. Did you know that if you read Psalm 22, written by David centuries before Jesus was born, you will read a description of the crucifixion of Jesus Christ that is written like a man who is standing at the foot of the cross? It tells about the piercing of His hands and feet, the gambling for His garments, the very words that Jesus would say upon the cross. Jesus wasn't looking back and quoting David; rather David was looking forward and quoting Jesus. It is an amazing thing that it is written as if somebody is an eyewitness to Christ's crucifixion.

This one psalm contains thirty-three direct prophecies that were fulfilled at Calvary, yet written a thousand years before the birth of Christ. And even more intriguing, when David wrote this prophecy, the form of capital punishment practiced by the Jews was stoning, not crucifixion. The Romans had not even come into power. Crucifixion was a Roman form of execution, and yet you find crucifixion described in Psalm 22.

Did He arrange that He would be crucified between two thieves? The Bible prophesied all of this in Isaiah 53:9–12; it was fulfilled as recorded in Matthew 27. The Bible prophesied that Judas would betray Him for exactly thirty pieces of silver in Zechariah 11:12. You can read about the fulfillment in Matthew 26:15.

And here is the classic "arrangement": He arranged to arise from the dead and be seen by more than five hundred witnesses. Some claim the apostles were hallucinating. Five hundred hallucinating at the same time? Having the same hallucination? Are people willing to die for a lie? No. People might live for a lie, but nobody will willingly die for a lie if they know that it is a lie. The early followers laid down their lives for the faith.

Most of these prophecies were not fulfilled by His friends but by His enemies, those who had the most to lose by the fulfillment of these prophecies. Matthew 26:56: "But all this was done that the Scriptures of the prophets might be fulfilled." Fulfilled prophecy is an incredible proof of the inspiration of the Bible.

The Bible Is Shown to Be the Word of God Because of Its Ever-Living Quality

The Bible is not the Book of the Month; it is the Book of the Ages. There is no book that has had as much opposition as the Bible. Men have laughed at it, they have scorned it, they have ridiculed it, they have made laws against it. There was a time in Scottish history when to own a Bible was a crime worthy of death. There are those who have vowed and declared that they will destroy this Book.

Peter declares, "All flesh is as grass, and all the glory of man as the flower of grass." You and I are just like a blade of grass sitting here; we are going to wither and die. "But the word of the Lord endures forever" (1 Pet. 1:24–25). Forever! We have some theological experts who think they have been called upon to reexamine the Bible. As far as I'm concerned, we ought to reexamine them. The Word of the Lord endures forever. The Bible is to judge us; we're not to judge the Bible. If you throw the old Book in the fiery furnace, it will come out without even the smell of smoke in its clothes.

Here we are in a new and a modern age, and we are still studying this old, old Book. It has stood the test of time and towers over all other books. God has kept the promise made to Isaiah more than twenty-five hundred years ago: "'As for Me,' says the LORD, 'this is My covenant with them: My Spirit who is upon you, and My words which I have put in your mouth, shall not depart from your mouth, nor from the mouth of your descendants, nor from the mouth of your descendants' descendants,' says the LORD, 'from this time and forevermore'" (Isa. 59:21).

The Bible Is Shown to Be the Word of God Because of Its Transforming Power

Finally, let's consider the transforming power of the Word of God. It is a compelling reason you can be certain the Bible is the Word of God. The great apostle Paul said in Romans 1:16, "For I am not ashamed of the gospel of Christ, for it is the power of God unto salvation." Hebrews 4:12 (KJV) says, "For the word of God is *quick* and powerful." That word *quick* is the word we get *zoo* and *zoology* from. It means it is alive; it pulsates with life and power. "The word of God is quick and *powerful.*" The word *powerful* is the word *energes,* the word we get *energy* from. There's life and there's energy in the Bible. We read other books while this Book reads us. It is incredible. It is saving to the sinner. I have used this Book so many times to lead people to Christ and have seen them transformed.

Billy Graham started his ministry as a young man, and often when he preached, he would say, "The Bible says, ... the Bible says." In 1954, he went to London to preach in the great Harringay Arena. A great crowd was there, including many news reporters. Two men who had come to see the flamboyant American evangelist were sitting up in the stands and discussing Billy Graham. One of the men was a medical doctor. They were finding fault with most everything.

Yet when Billy Graham began to preach, the Word of God began to take its toll. God says, "Is not My word ... like a hammer that breaks the rock in pieces?" (Jer. 23:29). The hammer began to fall and conviction fell on that place, and that medical doctor who had been ridiculing Billy Graham said to the man sitting next to him: "I don't know about you, but I'm going down there to give my heart to Christ." And the man next to him said, "Yes, and I'll go with you, and here's your billfold, I'm a pickpocket."

Later Graham stated, "I found in my preaching that the Word of God was like a rapier; and when I quoted it under the power of the Holy Spirit, I could slay everything before me."

That's the incredible power of the Word of God to "rescue the perishing" and "care for the dying" and "snatch them in pity from sin and the grave." I *know* personally the transforming power of the Word of God—it's changed my life.

- It is saving for the sinner. It will stir the conscience, convict the mind, and convert the soul.
- It is sweet for the saint. So many times I have found treasure and peace in the Word of God. Oh, how precious are the words of God.
- It is sufficient for the sufferer. How many times people have pillowed their head on the precious promises of the Word of God. I feel sorry for people who do not have a Bible to lean on.
- It is satisfying to the scholar. I have studied this Book, and I would never even dream of saying I've come to the bottom of the Word of God. Someone said the Word of God is so deep that the scholars can swim and never touch bottom and yet so precious that a little child can

come and get a drink without fear of drowning. Thank God for the Bible, the Word of God.

You can trust the Bible. You will never be a great Christian until you come to the unshakable conviction that the Bible is the Word of God.

STUDY QUESTIONS

1. "Man has only three problems: sin, sorrow, and death." Which of these three troubles is the most acute in your life right now? How are you heeding the Bible's counsel on how to handle it? What other counsel are you tempted to follow and act upon?

2. What one or two observations from nature most astound you with their enormity, their complexity, their mystery, or their consistency? How do these speak to you of God's creative power and wisdom and the truth revealed about Him in Scripture?

3. What would be different about the Bible if it were comprised exclusively of teaching, commands, and instructions? Why do you think God chose to frame so much of His Word in the historical contexts and happenings of its day?

4. Various examples of religious writings were considered for inclusion in the canon of Scripture when it was being formed under God's direction. What qualities do you think made our sixty-six books stand out as being authoritative and inspired?

5. How do you see people getting bogged down in the details of biblical prophecy and missing the larger purposes of its warnings

and encouragements? What hope do you derive from what God reveals about coming events? What fears does it give you?

6. Name a recent time when a certain passage of Scripture struck you as being precisely tailored to a current, pressing need, as though God had been listening in on your private thoughts and conversations? How do you typically respond to these moments?

7. What have you come to understand about the Word of God in the past few months and years that you didn't know before? What do you still wish you knew? How are you keeping your heart open and available for Him to show you more?

2

Every Christian Ought to Know
the Assurance of Salvation

---

*Whoever believes that Jesus is the Christ is born of God, and
everyone who loves Him who begot also loves him who is
begotten of Him. By this we know that we love the children of
God, when we love God and keep His commandments. For
this is the love of God, that we keep His commandments. And
His commandments are not burdensome. For whatever is
born of God overcomes the world. And this is the victory that
has overcome the world—our faith. Who is he who overcomes
the world, but he who believes that Jesus is the Son of God?
This is He who came by water and blood—Jesus Christ; not
only by water, but by water and blood. And it is the Spirit
who bears witness, because the Spirit is truth. For there are
three that bear witness in heaven: the Father, the Word, and
the Holy Spirit; and these three are one. And there are three*

*that bear witness on earth: the Spirit, the water, and the
blood; and these three agree as one.*

*If we receive the witness of men, the witness of God is greater;
for this is the witness of God which He has testified of
His Son. He who believes in the Son of God has the witness
in himself; he who does not believe God has made Him
a liar, because he has not believed the testimony that God has
given of His Son. And this is the testimony: that God has
given us eternal life, and this life is in His Son. He who has
the Son has life; he who does not have the Son of God does
not have life. These things I have written to you who believe
in the name of the Son of God, that you may know
that you have eternal life.*

1 JOHN 5:1–13

One basic thing every Christian ought to know beyond the
shadow of any doubt is that he or she is saved. Now what does it
mean to be saved? First, it means that every sin is forgiven and
buried in the grave of God's forgetfulness. Second, it means that
Jesus Christ through the Holy Spirit comes to live in us—to give
us peace, power, and purpose. Third, it means that when we die
or when Jesus comes again, we are going home to heaven to be
with Him.

Every Christian needs the absolute assurance that he or she
has had this experience of salvation. It is much better to be a
shouting Christian than a doubting Christian. We ought not walk
around like a question mark with our heads bent over but like an
exclamation mark. We should not be saying, "I hope I am saved,"

or, "I think I am saved," but, "Praise God, I know that I know that I am saved."

You Can Know without a Doubt

I was making a ministry call in the hospital. A lady was dying, and I had been called to her bedside to pray for her. I asked her if she had the assurance of salvation. She answered, "No." I asked her if she wanted to be saved. She said, "Indeed I do." So I explained to her from the Word of God how to be saved, and then I led her in a prayer. She prayed and asked Jesus Christ to forgive her sins, to come into her heart and save her. Of course, I thought this was wonderful. Here was a precious lady who in just a little while is going into the presence of God, and now she has that blessed assurance of salvation.

I turned to some of her family members who were there and said, "Isn't it wonderful that she has been saved and is going to heaven?" Her son-in-law said, "Nobody can know that she is saved."

I took my Bible and turned to 1 John 5:13 and read, "These things I have written to you who believe in the name of the Son of God, that you may know that you have eternal life, and that you may continue to believe in the name of the Son of God." I asked the man, "Do you see the word *know* in that verse?" I said, "Of course, we can know that we have eternal life." Someone has well said, "If you could have salvation and not know it, you could lose it and not miss it." The truth of the matter is, if you have genuine salvation, you should know it; and if it is real, thank God you can never lose it.

When we are talking about the assurance of salvation, we are talking about something of vital importance. We are not talking about denominational preference, the height of the church steeple, or the color of the carpet. We are talking about the eternal destiny of the human soul. We are talking about your ever-living, never-dying soul. We ought to have absolute certainty about some things. To be victorious in your Christian life, you need to be able to say, "I know that I am saved. I know that I am heaven born and heaven bound."

Can You Be Saved and Have Doubts about It?

But is it possible to be saved and to have doubts about it? If it is not possible for the child of God to sometimes be beleaguered with doubts, then why did the apostle John write, "These things I have written to you who believe in the name of the Son of God that you may know that you have eternal life." Evidently some were having serious questions and doubts about their salvation. Perhaps others thought they were saved but were not truly saved.

Doubt doesn't necessarily mean that you haven't been saved. As a matter of fact, we only tend to doubt that which we believe. Doubt is to your spirit what pain is to your body. Pain doesn't mean that one is dead. Pain means that there is life but that something is wrong. A part of the body is not functioning as it ought.

And so doubt is possible but not profitable. I have never known of any Christian who was really effective in his or her service to the Lord who did not have the full assurance of his or her salvation. Yet we must admit that Christians can have doubts and still be saved. However, it seems to me that they are going to heaven second-class.

I Doubt You've Been Saved

One lady told an evangelist, "I have been saved for twenty-five years and never had a doubt." He said, "I doubt you have been saved." That would be like a person saying, "We have been married for twenty-five years and never had an argument." Indeed we may have doubts. Doubts are not good in salvation, nor are arguments good in marriage. Pain is not good in our bodies, but these are the facts of life.

But I remind you that if you are trying to live the Christian life with doubts, it is much like driving an automobile with the brakes on. You need to have not a hope-so, think-so, maybe-so but a wonderful know-so salvation.

In this chapter I am going to stay primarily in the little epistle of 1 John, and in that small book, John uses the word *know* or *known* thirty-eight times. John is writing that we might *know* that we have eternal life—so we can call it the Book of Assurance.

Assurance Begins with the New Birth

"Whoever believes that Jesus is the Christ is born of God, and everyone who loves Him who begot also loves him who is begotten of Him" (1 John 5:1).

Being born spiritually is much like being born physically. One thing about birth is that it makes a perfect example of salvation because all of us have experienced a physical birth and can relate to the facts of a birth.

John's Gospel gives us clear teaching about this birth:

> There was a man of the Pharisees named
> Nicodemus, a ruler of the Jews. This man came to
> Jesus by night and said to Him, "Rabbi, we know
> that You are a teacher come from God; for no one
> can do these signs that You do unless God is
> with him."
> Jesus answered and said to him, "Most
> assuredly, I say to you, unless one is born again, he
> cannot see the kingdom of God."
> Nicodemus said to Him, "How can a man be
> born when he is old? Can he enter a second time
> into his mother's womb and be born?"
> Jesus answered, "Most assuredly, I say to you,
> unless one is born of water and the Spirit, he
> cannot enter the kingdom of God. That which is
> born of the flesh is flesh, and that which is born of
> the Spirit is spirit. Do not marvel that I said to you,
> 'You must be born again.'" (John 3:1–7)

In this passage Jesus was talking to a religious man named Nicodemus. Nicodemus wanted to know about miracles. In essence Jesus told him that in order for him to understand miracles, he himself needed to become a miracle. He needed to be born again. He asked Jesus about this. In his answer to Nicodemus,

Jesus pointed out some things about the new birth that we need to understand for full assurance.

In a birth, a conception takes place. In verse 5, Jesus said that we are born of water and the Spirit in order to enter into the kingdom of God. Water speaks of the Word of God, and the Spirit means the Spirit of God. When the Spirit of God and the Word of God come together in the womb of faith, there is wonderful conception. It will not happen without our consent. We must provide the womb of faith.

In a birth, a continuation is involved. Verse 6 tells us that physical life is imparted by physical life, and spiritual life is imparted by spiritual life.

Parents do not manufacture babies in the true sense of the word. They pass on the life that has been given to them. Life is transmitted.

Likewise in the new birth, the life of God is transmitted into us. The term "born again" literally means "born from above." Salvation is not only getting man out of earth into heaven but *getting God out of heaven* into man through His Spirit.

In a birth, a character is produced. In the flesh we receive the nature of our fleshly parents. When the Spirit of God and the Word of God create in us something supernatural, we receive the character of a new being with a divine nature.

Christians are not just nice people; they are new creatures. We are not like a tadpole that becomes a frog. We are more like a frog who has become a prince by the kiss of grace.

In a birth, a completion transpires. A birth is a once-for-all experience in the natural realm and also in the spiritual realm.

When a baby is born in earthly society, a record is written down. In heaven a new name is written down in glory. This speaks of a completed fact.

It is important that we understand this because no one can ever be unborn. Even when one's body ceases to exist, the spirit of an individual goes on timeless, dateless, and measureless throughout all eternity.

In a birth a commencement occurs. A birth is a starting place. A little child is all tomorrows. He has no past. No policemen will be there ready to arrest a newborn baby for crimes he has done. When we come to Jesus, we are not yesterdays—we are all tomorrows.

Having said that, however, we then commence to grow. When the baby is born, it has all of the equipment that it will ever have. Now it needs to grow. What a blessing to discover, develop, and deploy what we've received in our new birth!

In a birth a certainty is expected. A birth is a definite experience. If I were to ask you this question, "Have you ever been born?" it would almost seem nonsensical to ask it. But suppose I did ask it, and you were to answer, "I hope so. I'm doing the best I can." Or even more ridiculous, you would say, "I have always been born."

No, there is indeed a certainty implied by a birth. There was a time when you were not born, and there was a time when you were.

Let's talk about our part in the new birth. We had no choice about our first birth, but we have one about our second birth. As I said previously, we provide the womb of faith. "Whoever believes that Jesus is the Christ is born of God" (1 John 5:1). The new birth takes place when we believe on the Lord Jesus Christ.

The crystal clear and classic passage that relates to this is Ephesians 2:8–9, which says, "For by grace you have been saved through faith, and that not of yourselves; it is the gift of God, not of works, lest anyone should boast."

This passage is so great because here the Scripture clearly delineates what saves us, and then in contradistinction so we can make no mistake at all about it, it speaks of what does not save us. Therefore, we can look at it, first of all, negatively and see what doesn't save and then positively and see what does.

These verses tell us that self and works do not save. "Not of yourself." "Not of works." That seems simple enough, doesn't it? But most people do not understand that simple concept. If you asked the average man on the street, "Are you going to heaven?" "Sure!" "Why?" "I'm doing the best I can." Think about that answer. I (self) am doing (works) the best I can.

God Is Not Santa Claus

Many think that God is like Santa Claus—making a list, checking it twice, finding out who's naughty or nice. Then they think one day at the judgment we will stand before Him and He is going to weigh the good we've done against the bad and see which side the balance comes down on. Most people believe they can behave themselves into heaven.

But look at our Scripture again clearly. "Not of yourselves ... not of works" (Eph. 2:8–9). It is not of self, and it is not of works. The devil doesn't give up easily and will encourage you to believe something like this: "Yes, I cannot work my way to heaven, but works will help. It is the grace of God *plus* what I do. I do my part and God does His."

We're Not Going to Heaven in a Rowboat

I've heard this illustration used by those who believe in works plus grace: If you were rowing across a stream in a rowboat and pulled on one oar—we will call that "works"—you go around in a circle. But if you pull on the other oar—we will call that "faith"—you go around in a circle in the opposite direction. But then with a wise look on their face, they say both oars—faith *and* works—will get you across the stream. That may sound like a good illustration, but it has a fatal flaw: *we are not going to heaven in a rowboat!* We are going to heaven by the grace of God. It is not of self, and it is not of works.

If you don't understand that, you will never have the assurance of your salvation. If one small part depends on you, you will never have assurance. If any of it depends on your works, you will never know if you have done enough. Get this into your heart and head; it is not of self and not of works.

Now look at Ephesians 2:8 again carefully. "For by grace you have been saved through faith." On the positive side, it is grace through faith.

Now what is grace? Grace is the characteristic of God's nature that makes God love sinners such as we. God does not love us because we are valuable; we are valuable because He loves us. That love is by His sheer grace. Grace is something we do not deserve at all. It is God's unmerited love and favor shown to sinners who deserve judgment.

Grace—God's Riches at Christ's Expense

Here is a way to help understand what *grace* means. Let's make an acrostic out of it: G-R-A-C-E, "God's Riches At Christ's Expense." That's grace. When you think of grace, think of Jesus dying in agony and blood upon the cross for undeserving sinners. We have nothing to commend us to God. We are sinners by birth, choice, and practice, but God loves us in spite of our sin, and that love is called grace.

Grace is one of the most beautiful words in our language. When people understand grace, they want to write songs about it, like "Amazing Grace."

Faith—Forsaking All I Trust Him

If grace is God's riches at Christ's expense, what is faith? Here is another acrostic: F-A-I-T-H, "Forsaking All I Trust Him." I forsake dependence on my good intentions, my good deeds, my own so-called sense of self-worth, and I also forsake my sin. I turn my back on sin and I trust Him. I put my faith where God has put my sins—on the Lord Jesus Christ.

This faith is not a mere intellectual belief; the demons believe and tremble (James 2:19). No, it is more than belief. It is commitment. I can believe an airplane can fly, but I don't truly trust it until I get in it.

Here is how salvation works and the new birth comes about. I put my faith in God's grace. It is not the faith that saves; it is the grace that saves. Faith just lays hold of that grace. Think of grace as God's hand of love reaching down from heaven, saying, "I love you. I want to save you." It is a nail-pierced hand because He has paid for our sins. Think of faith as your sin-stained hand, saying, "God, I need You. I want You." And when you put your hand of faith in God's hand of grace, that is salvation. "For by grace you have been saved through faith, and that not of yourselves; it is the gift of God."

Grace Is a Gift

If you pay anything for a gift, then it ceases to be a gift. Suppose you have a friend named Jim who tells you, "I am going to buy you a $50,000 automobile as a gift." He drives up in front of your house with that brand-new automobile. Suppose you were to say to him, "Jim, I can't let you do that. It is just too great a gift. Here is a quarter. Here is twenty-five cents; let me help pay for this thing." And so he pays $49,999.75, and you pay two bits. Now you are driving the car down the road, and someone says, "That is a nice car you have there." You say, "Yes, my friend Jim and I bought this car." That would be an insult to Jim, would it not?

A Disgrace to Grace

We must remember that we cannot take any praise or credit for our salvation. None whatsoever! It is all of God. It is a gift, and we cannot boast about it. There will be no peacocks strutting around in heaven. When we get to heaven, God gets all of the praise and all of the glory because of His marvelous, matchless, wonderful grace.

The Birthmarks of the Believer

We said that when we enter the kingdom it is through a new birth, and that comes about when we put our faith in the grace of God. John, in the epistle of 1 John, gives some traits of the twice born. We might call these the birthmarks of the believer. If we are born again, the evidence will be there. I want to take three of these evidences that John mentions in this small epistle. You may test your salvation by them.

Number 1. The Commandment Test

"Now by this we know that we know Him, if we keep His commandments. He who says, 'I know Him,' and does not keep His commandments, is a liar, and the truth is not in him. But whoever keeps His word, truly the love of God is perfected in him. By this we know that we are in Him. He who says he abides in Him ought himself also to walk just as He walked" (1 John 2:3–6).

John does not beat around the bush here. He says in effect, "Look, don't tell me you are saved if you are not keeping God's commandments. If you say you are, you are a liar."

Let me be clear. You are not saved because you keep the commandments, but you will keep the commandments if you are saved. We have learned already that salvation is not of works. You are not saved by "commandment keeping."

Now that brings up a serious problem because there is not a one of us who would dare say that since we have been saved we have always obeyed every commandment to perfection.

Keeping the Stars

The understanding of all this is that word *keep*. It comes from the Greek word *tereō,* and among its meanings is "to watch over." It was used in ancient times by sailors. Those early sailors did not have global positioning satellites and radio signals to guide them, yet they sailed over the trackless seas. In doing that they sailed by the stars. They kept their eye on the heavens, and they called that "keeping the stars."

Keeping the stars is much like keeping the commandments. Any sailor could occasionally get blown off course, get distracted and waver this way or that. Yet he is keeping the stars.

When we keep the commandments, we steer by them. That does not speak of sinless perfection because none is perfect except Jesus Christ. But it does mean that our heart's desire is to keep the Word of God. From the moment I gave my heart to Jesus Christ, there has been in me a desire to keep God's Word.

There are a couple more problem verses in 1 John. We might as well look at them full on. "Whoever abides in Him does not sin. Whoever sins has neither seen Him nor known Him" (1 John 3:6).

"He who sins is of the devil, for the devil has sinned from the beginning. For this purpose the Son of God was manifested, that He might destroy the works of the devil. Whoever has been born of God does not sin, for His seed remains in him; and he cannot sin, because he has been born of God" (1 John 3:8–9).

You might say, "I must not be saved because I know that the ability to sin is within me." Again we have to do a little study because there is an adequate answer. "He who sins" is in the present tense, and it speaks of a habitual course of action. John is saying that a man who is born of God does not make sin his practice, his lifestyle, his habit. It does not mean that he could not slip into sin.

May I give this testimony? Before I was saved, I was running to sin. Since being saved, I am running from it. I may fall, I may slip, I may fail, but my heart's desire is to live for God.

John is saying, "If you call yourself a Christian and you are not steering by God's commandments, and if you are living a habitually sinful life with no conviction, no compunction, no contrition, no disquietude, then don't call yourself a Christian because you are not."

Number 2. The Companion Test

"We know that we have passed from death to life, because we love the brethren. He who does not love his brother abides in death. Whoever hates his brother is a murderer, and you know that no murderer has eternal life abiding in him" (1 John 3:14–15).

Remember that when we believe on the Lord Jesus Christ, we are born of God. Remember that we have a new nature, and it is God's nature. Also remember that we are in the family of God, and so we have brothers and sisters.

So if I am born of God and have become a partaker of His divine nature, love will automatically be in my heart, for God is love. To be God's child is to share God's nature. We don't need a bumper sticker or a lapel pin to prove that we are Christians. Jesus said, "By this will all men know that you are My disciples if you have love for one another" (John 13:35 NASB).

Love is the nature of God, and therefore it is characteristic of His children. If we love Him and His love is in us, then we are going to love what He loves, which is His dear family. This is the reason it is foolish to say yes to Jesus but no to His church. Many descriptions and analogies describe the church:

- The church is a **building**, and Christ is the foundation. Who could say yes to the foundation and no to the building that rests upon it?
- The church is His **bride**. Who could say yes to the groom and no to the bride?
- The church is His **body**. Who could say yes to Christ the head and then no to the body?

So one of the marks, the traits of the twice born, is that we love one another—the members of His church.

That doesn't mean that we are all lovable by nature. We are not by nature lovely. We are sinners. A church is comprised of people who have finally realized that they are sinners and banded themselves together to do something about it. It is the only organization I know of besides Hell's Angels that you have to profess to be bad before you can join. One must say, "I am a sinner, and I am turning my life over to Jesus Christ."

Therefore, all of us are in various stages in our spiritual growth and sanctification. Those in the church with us who are steering by the stars may be temporarily off course, they may fail, but they are onboard with us, and they are our brothers and sisters. To love Jesus is to love His church. To persecute His church is to persecute Jesus.

A man named Saul, who later became the apostle Paul, was on the road to Damascus to arrest Christians. The Lord Jesus appeared to him in a blinding light and said, "Saul, Saul, why are you persecuting Me?" Saul could have said, "Whoever you are, I am not persecuting you; I am persecuting the church." The truth of the matter is, however, that when one persecutes the church, he is persecuting Jesus. To neglect the church is to neglect Jesus; to love the church is to love Jesus. That kind of love is a birthmark of the believer.

Number 3. The Confidence Test

"He who believes in the Son of God has the witness in himself; he who does not believe God has made Him a liar, because he has not believed the testimony that God has given of His Son" (1 John 5:10). This is the greatest and strongest test. All of the others grow out of it.

Biblical belief (confidence) is not just an intellectual exercise. You do not believe *about* Jesus; you believe *in* Jesus. You can believe an airplane can fly, but you trust it when you get onboard. Again I remind you that it is more than an intellectual assent to some facts that saves us.

Notice also that this verse is in the present tense. It doesn't say, "He who has believed"; it says, "He who *believes.*" Our confidence is always to be in the present tense.

Sometimes the question is asked, "Are you saved?" The answer comes, "Yes I am saved. I remember walking down the aisle when I was nine years old, giving my hand to my pastor and my heart to Jesus Christ. I may not be living for God right now. I'll admit that. But I know I'm saved because I remember what I did when I was a nine-year-old boy. I remember believing on Jesus Christ."

The Bible never uses such an experience as proof of salvation. It never points us back to some time when we may have believed on Jesus Christ. It always deals with our present confidence.

It is interesting how many people want to go back to an event in the past. Some even say, "If you cannot show me the place and tell me the moment when you received Jesus Christ as your personal Savior and Lord, then you are not saved." There is just one thing wrong with that; it is not biblical and not so.

The Bible never says that you will know you are saved by something you remember in the past. It says, "He that believes." Present tense! It is simple. If you are believing, you did believe.

The question is, Are you believing in Jesus right now? Some true believers are concerned because they cannot remember the exact time like others can. Some had a cataclysmic experience when they turned in faith from sin to Christ. Others grew up in a Christian family and were nurtured along until one day it dawned on them that they were trusting Jesus as their personal Lord and Savior. That doesn't mean they were half saved and then three-quarters saved and then all the way saved. No one is half saved. To be half saved is to be altogether lost. There was a time when they came to saving faith, but they may not be able to pinpoint that particular time like others can do.

How Do We Know We Are in Georgia?

Let me illustrate. Suppose we are both in Orlando, Florida, and we are going to Atlanta, Georgia. You drive to Atlanta and I fly. I ask you to meet me in Atlanta and to pick me up at the airport. When you drive, you will know when you cross the state line. It will be obvious because a sign will be there that says, "Welcome to Georgia." When I fly, I will cross the same line, but I will not be aware of it. But I will land in the Atlanta airport. We meet in the Atlanta airport, and we are both there. I came in an airplane, and you came in an automobile. You give your testimony and say, "I remember exactly when I crossed the state line." My testimony is, "I don't remember when I crossed the state line, but I know I did because I am in the Atlanta airport. The important thing is that *since* I am in the Atlanta airport, I know I *must* be in Georgia and *did* cross that line."

If you *are* trusting Jesus, you *did* trust Jesus. The real test is not whether you remember the time or the place but that you are this moment putting your confidence in the Lord Jesus Christ.

The story is told of Will Rogers who one time went in to get a passport, and the official said, "We need your birth certificate." And he said, "What for?" They said, "For proof of your birth." He said, "Well I'm here, ain't I?" That makes the point for me. If you *are* trusting Jesus—present tense—you are saved. If not, don't rely on some past experience.

This brings another question. How can we know if we are truly believing at this moment?

The Witness of the Spirit

First, there is the witness of the Spirit. "He who believes in the Son of God has the witness in himself" (1 John 5:10). The witness of the Spirit is not an emotional feeling. Your emotions are the shallowest part of your nature. Salvation is the deepest work of God. He will not do the deepest work in the shallowest part. The witness of the Spirit is the Holy Spirit speaking to your human spirit with a quiet confidence that you belong to Jesus Christ. It is an inner awareness that those who are saved know that they are. A true believer with this witness is never at the mercy of an unbeliever who has an argument.

The Witness of the Word

The second witness is the witness of the Word. "And this is the testimony: that God has given us eternal life, and this life is in His Son. He who has the Son has life; he who does not have the Son of God does not have life. These things I have *written to you who believe* in the name of the Son of God, that you may *know* that you have eternal life" (1 John 5:11–13). The Scripture is given to us that we may know.

One night while out sharing Jesus Christ, I asked a man if he wanted to receive Christ as his personal Lord and Savior. He did, and after we prayed together, I said, "I want to give you your spiritual birth certificate." I turned to John 5:24 and read, "Most assuredly, I say to you, he who hears My word and believes in Him who sent Me has everlasting life, and shall not come into judgment, but has passed from death into life."

I read it slowly and said, "This is Jesus who is speaking. Do you believe this?"

"Yes," he said.

"'He who hears My word.' Have you heard His word?"

"Yes."

"'And believes in Him who sent Me.' Have you believed on the God that sent the Lord Jesus?"

"Yes."

"'Has everlasting life.' Do you have everlasting life?"

"I hope so," he said.

I said, "Let's read it again." And we did. Again he answered yes to every question but the last. Again he said, "I hope so." "Let's read it again," I said. This time when I asked him if he had everlasting life, the light went on inside. "Why, yes! Yes!" he shouted. "Who says so?" "God says so! God says so!" That is the confidence of the Word. Put them together; the witness of the Spirit and the witness of the Scripture give us this glad certainty.

Let me say before you read any further that if you have never received Jesus Christ as your personal Lord and Savior, you may do so right now. By an act of faith, trust Him to save you. He is ready and willing and will do it this very moment. Don't look for a sign and don't ask for a feeling; stand on His Word.

If you are saved and have doubts, don't look back to some past experience. Ask yourself this moment: Am I trusting Jesus? If not, trust Him right now. If you are trusting, there will be the genuine birthmarks in your life. There will be a desire to obey His commandments, there will be a love for His people, and there will be a quiet confidence witnessed by the Holy Spirit and the Bible that you belong to Him.

My Personal Testimony

As a young teen I gave my heart to Christ, but I did not have it explained to me as I have explained it to you. For some months I was up and down. I didn't know whether I was lost and the Holy

Spirit had me under conviction or I was saved and the devil was trying to make me doubt it.

I had walked my girlfriend home and stopped at the corner of Calvin Avenue and 39th Street in West Palm Beach, Florida. I wanted to get it settled. I looked up into the starry sky, wanting to look into the face of God. I said, "O God, I don't have assurance. I am going to get it settled tonight, once and for all, now and forever."

I prayed this way, "Lord Jesus, with all my heart, I trust You to save me. I don't look for a sign, and I don't ask for a feeling. I stand on Your Word and You cannot lie. I trust You to save me." I continued to pray, "Lord, if I was saved before, this can't take it away, but if I wasn't, I am driving down a peg tonight. This settles it forever." A river of peace started to flow in my heart, and it is still flowing right now.

Blessed Assurance

If you do that and still have doubts, do you know what is probably wrong? You have got some sin in your life. You are not obeying the Lord, and you need to confess that sin because there is nothing more damaging to faith and confidence than unconfessed, unrepented sin in your heart and in your life. Deal with that sin and see if the confidence of your salvation does not return!

Thank God for a know-so salvation.

STUDY QUESTIONS

1. What are some of the doubts you've felt or experienced as you've thought about the certainty of your salvation? Where do

these doubts tend to lead you? What harm have they caused, and what might you be missing by not feeling free to let them go?

2. Which of the quite logical conclusions about *birth* presented in chapter 2 is the most compelling to you in terms of understanding what it means to be "born again" or spiritually reborn? How does this argument alleviate some of your lingering doubts?

3. What are some of the faulty beliefs about the nature of God and His grace that you brought with you from your earliest teachings or feelings about Him? How has His Word challenged and transformed your grasp of who He is and why He loves you?

4. How do you tend to react to the sin in your life, even after being delivered through Christ from its power over you? What would you identify as the main culprits behind your most habitual slip-ups into sinful decisions and rash behaviors?

5. What have been some of your biggest areas of disillusionment with the church? What seems like the best way to respond to these? Why might we expect the church to contain some of the same kinds of conflict and difficulty we experience in other relationships?

6. Why do you think God may have led you into saving relationship with Him in a different way than He chose to lead others? Could most of the questions about your salvation simply be distractions keeping you from enjoying the freedom of abundant life?

7. How do you intend to keep growing in your Christian faith, trusting Him with greater surrender, being used by Him for greater avenues of service, desiring that your life reflect His glory no matter what circumstances He allows into your life?

3

Every Christian Ought to Know
about Eternal Security

My sheep hear My voice, and I know them, and they follow Me. And I give them eternal life, and they shall never perish; neither shall anyone snatch them out of My hand. My Father, who has given them to Me, is greater than all; and no one is able to snatch them out of My Father's hand.

John 10:27–29

Is there anything better than being saved? Now, be careful how you answer because it's a loaded question. Yes, there's something better than being saved: It is being saved and knowing that you're saved, having that blessed assurance. Well, is there anything better than being saved and knowing you're saved? Yes, there is! It is being saved, knowing that you're saved, and knowing that you can never *ever* lose your salvation.

If that proposition is true, you will have to admit that is indeed wonderful: That you could be saved—heaven born and heaven bound, that you can have the absolute assurance that you're saved, and that you can know that you can never ever lose your salvation. Well, I want to show you that, indeed, it is true!

Sometimes eternal security is looked upon as a denominational doctrine. Let's go past that. It doesn't make any difference what any denomination believes if it is not Bible based. We're going to see what the Bible has to say about eternal security. If the Bible says it, we're going to believe it. If the Bible doesn't say it, then we have no authority to believe it. The doctrine of eternal security is not incidental; it is absolutely fundamental to your Christian life for several reasons.

Spiritual Health

First, you need to have this assurance for your spiritual health. Can you imagine a little child in a family who does not know from one day to the next whether he may be in the family? Perhaps one day he was naughty and disobeyed, and so he's no longer a member of the family. Then after several weeks he repents and gets right again, and he is received back into the family. He has his bedroom again, and he can see his mother and daddy again and brother and sister again. Then after a while he's out of the family again—that's not my daddy, that's not my mother, that's not my brother, that's not my sister, that's not my house. Can you imagine what an emotional wreck the child would be if he went through that?

I know Christians who are emotional wrecks because they do not have the assurance that they are children of God. They're in the family and then out of the family, then in the family and out of the family.

Your Productivity

I know few Christians who are spiritually productive who do not have the assurance of their salvation and understand that they are eternally secure. Why is this? Very simple—when we know that the future is secure, then we can concentrate on the present.

In 1937, the Golden Gate Bridge was built in San Francisco, spanning that great bay. I have seen that bridge; it's a marvel and a wonder. It was a dangerous, treacherous thing to work on that bridge, as it began to rise hundreds of feet above the icy swirling waters of San Francisco Bay. The workmen were afraid for their lives. Some of them fell and drowned; in all, twenty-three people there lost their lives in accidental deaths.

Management said, "We've got to do something about that," so they built a safety net underneath the workers. They spent $100,000 building this net, and when they built the safety net, they found out it really wasn't an expense. It was a great saving, because the work went 25 percent faster, and far fewer lives were lost. As a matter of fact, only ten, fewer than half as many, fell in the net, and of course their lives were saved.

Why could these people work with more productivity? Because of their security! They knew that the net was there. And that's the way it is in the Christian life.

I'm not endeavoring to keep myself safe; I know I am saved. I'm saved by the grace of God; therefore I can be productive with grateful service. *When we are confident of the future, we can concentrate on the present.*

Aid in Evangelism

A lot of people would like to be saved, but they think, *Well, I just can't live it. I can't hold out. I know how weak I am.* They're just afraid that they would go forward in the church, profess to be a Christian, and then fall away and look foolish.

How wonderful to tell these people that the God who saves them is the God who will keep them. It's a great tool in evangelism—sharing the Lord Jesus Christ.

They Never Were a Christian in the First Place

What do we mean by *eternal security*? We don't mean that once a person joins a church and gets baptized she's eternally secure because she may or may not be saved. We're talking about somebody who has become a partaker of the divine nature, somebody who is heaven born and therefore heaven bound, a person who has had a new birth, a person who has become genuinely a child of God.

Sometimes when I teach on this subject of the new birth, somebody will say, "I know somebody who used to be a Christian who is no longer a Christian." I just say, "Well, you think you know somebody who used to be a Christian and is no longer a Christian. Maybe he never was a Christian, or maybe he still is a Christian. You are not equipped to judge."

I Never Knew You

Many people look like Christians and act like Christians, but they've never been saved. An interesting verse is Matthew 7:22. Jesus is talking about the final judgment: "Many will say to Me in that day, 'Lord, Lord [Now that's the proper profession; they call him Lord!], have we not prophesied in Your name [The word *prophesy* means to speak for God; evidently these were preachers!], cast out demons in Your name [claiming that they were exorcising demons from people], and done many wonders in Your name?'" [Maybe they sang in the choir, took up the offering, or taught Sunday school.] And then Jesus says in the next verse, "And then will I declare to them, 'I never knew you; depart from Me, you who practice lawlessness!'" He didn't say, "Oh, you had it, but you lost it." He says instead, "I *never* knew you."

You say that person used to be a Christian and no longer is because you heard him prophesy, you saw him do all these wonderful works. But he didn't lose his salvation. He never had it!

Let me give you a verse in contradistinction to Matthew 7:22–23. It's John 10:27–28. Jesus said, "My sheep hear My voice, and I know them, and they follow Me." In the Matthew passage He said, "I never knew you." This time He says, "My sheep hear My voice, and I know them, and they follow Me. And I give them eternal life, and they shall never perish." You see the difference: Some are religious, but they never were saved; the others were saved, and they will never perish. Those who fall away never were truly saved.

Another key verse is 1 John 2:19. It talks about those who begin for a while and then they go away from the faith. This verse explains it: "They went out from us, but they were not of us; for if they had been of us, they would [no doubt] have continued with us; but they went out that they might be made manifest, that none of them were of us." These people start out for God, continue awhile, and then they go back to the old way. Somebody says, "They lost their salvation." John says, "No, they went out from us because they were not of us. Had they been of us, they would no doubt have continued with us." Here's a saying I like that sums it up:

> *The faith that fizzles before the finish*
> *had a flaw from the first.*

They never really knew the Lord.

I want to give you some reasons I believe in the eternal security of the believer.

God's Sacred Promise

God has made a sacred promise to you. It is found in Romans 8:38–39. This is going to be one of the most all-inclusive statements you will ever read—in the Bible or out of the Bible. Pay close attention. Paul is going to tell us ten strong opponents that can never separate us from God's love. "For I am persuaded that neither death nor life, nor angels nor principalities nor powers, nor things present nor things to come, nor height nor depth, nor any other created thing, shall be able to separate us from the love of God which is in Christ Jesus our Lord."

Notice these opponents:

- Death
- Life
- Angels
- Principalities
- Powers
- Things present
- Things to come
- Height
- Depth
- Any other creature

That's powerful, isn't it? He is saying there is *nothing* that can separate us from the love of God. That is a sacred promise. It is a wonderfully inclusive verse.

I challenge you, the reader, to name any force that may separate us from God's love that Paul failed to mention.

God's Determined Purpose

In Philippians 1:6, the apostle Paul says this: "Being confident of this very thing, that He who has begun a good work in you will complete it." Paul was confident of this—that which God starts, He will finish. God is the One who saves us. Salvation is the work of God; it is not "do it yourself." Who began a good work in us? The Holy Spirit of God! He was the *Convictor.* Do you think that you were convicted of your sin by yourself? No, the Bible says, "There is none who seeks after God" (Rom. 3:11). He's the One who ran you down and convicted you of your sin. If He couldn't run faster than you could run, you never would have been saved. "We love Him because He first loved us" (1 John 4:19).

Not only is He the Convictor, but also He is the *Convertor.* He was the one who opened our understanding. That's the reason I pray before I preach. Anything I can talk you into, somebody else can talk you out of. Anything that the Holy Spirit gives you is yours.

He is the Convictor and the Convertor, and therefore, He is the *Completor.* Have you ever started anything you couldn't finish? When I was a little boy, I used to build model airplanes. I don't think I ever finished one of them. That's just a character flaw on my part. Many of us start things we just can't finish.

I heard one time that Billy and Jimmy were talking, and Billy said to Jimmy, "My daddy has a list of men that he can whip, and your dad's name is number one on the list." Jimmy went home and told his daddy, "Daddy, did you know that Billy's dad has a list of men that he can whip, and your name is number one on the list?" Jimmy's daddy said, "Is that so?" Jimmy said, "That's what I heard." Jimmy's daddy went over to Billy's daddy and knocked on the door. Jimmy's daddy said, "My son Jimmy said that your son Billy said that you have a list of men you can whip, and my name is number one on that list. Is that right?" Billy's daddy said, "Yes, that's right." Jimmy's daddy said, "Well, I don't believe you can do it. What are you going to do about that?" Billy's daddy said, "Well, I'll just take your name off the list."

God never has to take our name off the list. God never starts something that He can't finish. I thank God for that. Look at this verse again: "Being confident of this very thing, that He who has begun a good work in you will complete it." If salvation is *your* work, maybe it will run out in a ditch somewhere; but if it's *God's* work, it will be completed. It's wonderful. Let me give you another reason.

God's Sovereign Predestination

You are already predestined to be like Jesus. We're in deep theology here, but let's see what the Bible says in Romans 8:29–30: "For whom He foreknew [He knew you were going to be saved before you were ever saved], He also predestined to be conformed to the image of His Son, that He might be the firstborn among many brethren. Moreover whom He predestined, these He also called; whom He called, these He also justified; and whom He justified, these He also glorified."

God has a plan for you: you're going to be like Jesus. God looked before you were ever born. He saw you receiving Christ as your personal Savior and Lord. He said, "That one's going to be like Jesus." "For whom He foreknew, He also predestined." Do you know what "predestined" means? It means your destiny is already determined. You are predestined to be like Jesus. If you're predestined to be like Jesus, will you be like Jesus? (It's all right to say yes. It would be wrong to say no.) If you're predestined to be like Jesus, *of course* you will be like Jesus. What is foreknown in heaven cannot be annulled by hell. It's predestined; *it is settled!*

Read the verse again: "For whom He foreknew [He knew you were going to be saved before you were ever saved.], He also predestined to be conformed to the image of His Son, that He might be the firstborn among many brethren. Moreover whom He predestined, these He also called; whom He called, these He also justified; and whom He justified, these He also glorified." We would expect him to say, "He will glorify." However, God already sees you glorified before it happens because we live *in* history, but He lives *above and beyond* history. God sees you already glorified in heaven. Well, if that is true, and it is true of course, obviously you're predestined to be like the Lord Jesus Christ.

You might say, "I don't feel so glorified right now." He's not finished with you. But He has begun a good work, and what He has begun, He will complete. You are predestined—if you are a believer—to be like the Lord Jesus Christ.

Calvary's Perfect Provision

The Bible says something wonderful in Hebrews 10:14: "For by one offering He [the Lord] has perfected forever those who are being sanctified." Notice the phrase "perfected forever." Jesus Christ hung upon that cross in agony never to die again. His one offering perfected forever those of us who are saved. Because of the perfect Sacrifice, we have complete perfection in the Lord Jesus Christ. When you get saved, God doesn't just give you a fresh start; He gives you eternal perfection by that "one offering."

Nowhere in the Bible can you find where anybody is ever saved twice. You can't find it. You couldn't find where anybody was saved twice any more than you could find where anybody was born physically two times. You're born physically once, and you're born spiritually once. You never find that being repeated. Why? Because "by one offering He has perfected [us] forever." When you were saved, you were stamped with a stamp that said, "Good for one salvation only." If you were to lose that salvation, Jesus would have to die again for you to be saved again. You're saved as many times as Jesus died. "For by *one* offering He has perfected forever."

Now somebody may say, "Well, what if I sin after I am saved?" We've all sinned since we've been saved. Jesus is a Savior, not a probation officer. If I depend on my behavior to keep me saved, then I'll be hopelessly lost. If you were to follow me around, you might say, "Oh, he doesn't sin." But you'd make a mistake. I don't steal, I don't commit adultery, I don't use God's name in vain, I don't tell lies. But do you know how the Bible defines sin? The Bible says, "To him who knows to do good and does not do it, to him it is sin" (James 4:17). I don't always do everything I know I ought to do. The Bible says, "The thought of foolishness is sin" (Prov. 24:9 KJV). The Bible says, "Whatsoever is not of faith is sin" (Rom. 14:23 KJV). Do I have perfect faith about everything? No, I'm sad to say.

I wouldn't trust the best fifteen minutes I ever lived to get me to heaven, much less some of my bad ones. And so if I have to depend on my behavior to get me to heaven, I'm not going to make it, and you're not going to make it, and no one is going to make it.

Let me show you a wonderful Scripture, Romans 4:5: "But to him who does not work but believes on Him who justifies the ungodly, his faith is accounted for righteousness." God doesn't say that I'm righteous because of my good works but because I put my faith where God put my sins—on Jesus. Notice what follows: "Just as David also describes the blessedness of the man to whom God imputes righteousness apart from works." Do you know what the word *impute* means? It means to put on one's account. When somebody has something added to their account in Bible terms, it's imputed to them. The next time you go to the department store to buy something, if you want to have a little fun with the clerk, don't say, "Charge it," just say, "Impute it." It means the same thing: "Put that on my account."

When you got saved, God wrote "righteous" on your account. You didn't earn it. Blessed is "the man to whom God imputes righteousness apart from works." God put it on your account apart from your good deeds.

It gets even sweeter. Verse 7 says, "Blessed are those whose lawless deeds are forgiven, and whose sins are covered." Now, watch this: we put our faith in Christ; God calls us righteous. He puts that righteousness on our account without any works of our own, and then it says, "Blessed are those whose lawless deeds are forgiven." That's great!

If you stole ten dollars from me, and you came up to me and said, "I'm sorry, I stole ten dollars from you. Here's the ten dollars," and then you say, "Will you forgive me?" I may say, "Sure, I'll forgive you," but I couldn't cleanse you. You still stole it. All I can do is forgive you. But this Scripture says, "Whose lawless deeds are forgiven, and whose sins are covered." *Covered* means they're blotted out as if it never happened.

But it even gets better. Look at verse 8: "Blessed is the man [now here's the shouting part] to whom the LORD shall not impute sin." Not only does He impute righteousness, not only does He forgive, not only does He blot out my sins, but also the Scripture says, "The LORD shall not impute sin." If God were to put one-half of one sin on my account, I'd be lost forever. If we're depending on ourselves for our security, we'll never have it.

You say, "Well, I did pretty good today, but I did lose my temper in traffic, and I was cross with my child; I did kick the cat. Maybe I won't make it." No, friend, this is a wonderful salvation because it is of God.

Remember Calvary's perfect provision. Nobody is saved twice because Jesus died only once, "For by one offering He has perfected *forever* those who are being sanctified" (Heb. 10:14).

The Saint's New Position

What is your new position? When you get saved, it is in Christ Jesus. "Therefore, if anyone is in Christ, he is a new creation; old things have passed away; behold, all things have become new" (2 Cor. 5:17).

There are only two representative persons who've ever lived, and we're all part of one of those two persons—Adam or Christ. In Adam all die. In Christ all are made alive. Everybody is either in Adam or in Christ.

If you're in Christ, that is your new position, and what pertains to Jesus pertains to you. You are in Christ. The only way you could lose your salvation would be for Christ to lose His relationship with the Father because you are in Christ. You are a part of the body of Christ. It is unthinkable that a part of the body of Christ should perish.

A Little "Ark"eology

Because He wants us to understand salvation, God gives many illustrations and object lessons in the Bible. Noah's ark is one of these object lessons of salvation. Peter tells us that the ark is a picture, a type of the Lord Jesus Christ (1 Pet. 3:18–22). I want to see what kind of Bible scholar you are, so I'm going to tell you the story of the ark, and you check me to see if I get it correct.

God said, "Noah, the way people are living is a disgrace, and I'm sorry that I made mankind. I'm going to destroy them with a flood, so, Noah, you build this ark. I'll give you the dimensions; I'll show you how to build it. And after you've gotten it built, Noah, I want you to put some pegs on the side of that ark for you to hold on to. Put eight pegs there—one for yourself and one for Mrs. Noah, one for Shem, one for Ham, one for Japheth, and one for their wives.

"And when the flood starts, Noah, you get a stepladder, get up there and get hold of one of those pegs. And hold on with all your might because it's going to be a rough ride. And Noah, if you can hold on until the water goes down, you'll be safe."

And Noah got hold of one of those little slimy pegs and began to hold on. He looked over to his wife and said, "Sweetheart, you pray for me, that I'll hold out faithful to the end."

Is that the way it happened? Of course not. You know that's not the way it happened. God told Noah to make the ark, and the Bible says, "Then the LORD said to Noah, 'Come into the ark.'" He didn't say, "Go into the ark." He said, "Come into the ark" (Gen. 7:1).

If I'm *here* and I say, "You go *there*," that means you go where I'm not. If I'm *here* and say, "Come in *here*," that means you come where I am. Right? So God was in the ark. Had the ark gone down, God would have gone down. And then the Bible says, "And the LORD shut him in" (Gen. 7:16). Why did God shut the door? Two reasons—to shut the water out and to shut Noah in.

Noah and his family were in the ark. How safe was Noah? As safe as the ark. How safe am I? As safe as Jesus, who is my ark of safety. Noah may have fallen down inside the ark, but he never fell out of the ark because God *shut* him in, and God *sealed* him in!

The Bible says in the book of Ephesians that after we're saved, we are "sealed with the Holy Spirit of promise" (Eph. 1:13). We're sealed into the Lord Jesus Christ.

Hallelujah, I Made It!

A lot of folks believe in eternal security, but here's the kind of eternal security they believe in. They say, "Well, one of these days I'm going to get to heaven and say, 'I made it! Hallelujah! Here I am in heaven. Thank God I'm secure.' I'll slam the door behind me. I am safe in heaven." Well now, wait a minute. What makes you think you'll be secure in heaven? The angels fell from heaven. If you're not secure down here, you wouldn't be secure up there.

Security is not in a *place*; it's in a *person*. His name is Jesus! You are *in Christ*. Remember again God's promise in 2 Corinthians 5:17: "If anyone is in Christ, he is a new creation." So that's another reason you can know you are eternally secure—your position in Christ.

The Believer's Eternal Provision

In John 5:24 (KJV) Jesus is speaking, and here is the preface to what He says: "Verily, verily [now when Jesus says, 'Verily, verily,' it means 'Pay attention, pay attention; listen, listen'], I say unto you, He that heareth my word, and believeth on him that sent me, hath everlasting life, and shall not come into condemnation; but is passed from death unto life." Jesus said, "Listen, listen; pay attention. When you hear My word and believe on the God that sent Me to be the Savior of the world, you have everlasting life. You will not come into condemnation, you will not be judged, but you have already passed from death to life."

Question: When do you get eternal life? Do you get eternal life when you die and go to heaven? No! Sometimes you see a grave marker "Entered into Eternal Life." No, friend, if you don't have eternal life before you die, you're not going to get it when they put you in the ground. You get eternal life the moment you believe in Jesus Christ. That's what this Scripture says: "Verily, verily, I say unto you, he that heareth my word, and believeth on him that sent me, *hath* everlasting life [not *will* get], and shall not come into condemnation; but *is* passed from death unto life." Notice it says "*is* passed," not "*will* pass."

Do *you* have everlasting life? If you believe in Christ, you do. When did you get it? When you believed.

If you have everlasting life, will it ever end? Of course not, because it's everlasting. If it ends, whatever you had wasn't everlasting. Suppose you were a Christian for ten years and then you lost your salvation. What did you have? A ten-year life.

Suppose you were a Christian for fifty years and then lost it, what did you have? A fifty-year life. Friend, whatever it is that you have, if you ever lose it, whatever it was, it wasn't everlasting.

Jesus said, "I give them everlasting life," not that they will get it when they die. It is present tense. You have everlasting life now. Isn't that great? Sure, it's great; it's wonderful!

Jesus' Interceding Prayer

Jesus is praying for you. His high priestly prayer is in John 17:9. He was praying for His disciples, and here's what He prayed: "I pray for them. I do not pray for the world but for those whom You have given Me, for they are Yours." Jesus was praying for His apostles, for His disciples. What did He pray for them? "I do not pray that You should take them out of the world, but that You should keep them from the evil one" (John 17:15). He says, "Now Lord, I'm not asking that You take them immediately to heaven, but Father I pray that You'll keep them from the evil one."

In Luke 22 when Jesus said to Simon Peter, "Simon, Simon! Indeed, Satan has asked for you, that he may sift you as wheat. But I have prayed for you, that your faith should not fail" (vv. 31–32). Now, did Jesus ever pray a prayer that was not answered? Of course not! He said, "Father, I thank You that ... You *always* hear Me" (John 11:41). Why? He always prayed to do the will of the Father; He always prayed in faith; sin never inhibited His prayer. Every prayer that He prayed was answered, and He prayed for these disciples, "Father, I pray that You will keep them."

He said, "Peter, the devil wants to sift you like wheat. I'm going to allow him to do it because you need to understand what's in your heart. You need to understand something that needs to be sifted out. I'm going to allow him to do it, but I have prayed for you that your faith won't fail." And that same Peter who cursed and swore and denied Christ was the flaming apostle of Pentecost, who wrote two books in the New Testament because Jesus prayed for him.

You may say, "Yes, sure, Peter was prayed for, and James and Matthew and the rest of them, but Jesus never prayed for me like that." Well, in this same chapter, John 17:20, He says this: "I do not pray for these alone, but also for those who will believe in Me through their word." Just write your name down right there because He might as well have put your name there. Jesus has prayed that you're going to be kept. It was a prayer that transcends the centuries with a delayed detonation.

If He has prayed for you, will His prayer be answered? Absolutely! As a matter of fact, Hebrews 7:25 says, "Therefore He is also able to save to the uttermost those who come to God through Him, since He always lives to make intercession for them." "To save to the uttermost"—do you know what that means? To save all the way—to save you to the end because He's always making intercession for you. The finished work of Jesus is Calvary. He died on the cross and said, "It is finished." But the unfinished work is intercession. He is praying for you and for me, and that prayer is answered. He said, "Father, I thank You that You always hear Me."

God's Almighty Power

I have children and grandchildren, and I want to tell you this: If someone wanted to harm them and somebody wanted to snatch them away from their family, away from love, and destroy them, if I could, I would keep it from happening. Does that make sense to you? If I could, I would keep it from happening.

I'm only human. I don't have all power, but God is able to do it, and He has the power. "Blessed be the God and Father of our Lord Jesus Christ, who according to His abundant mercy has begotten us again to a living hope through the resurrection of Jesus Christ from the dead, to an inheritance incorruptible and undefiled that does not fade away, reserved in heaven for you" (1 Pet. 1:3–4).

Friend, there's a treasure laid up in glory for you, and the lawyers can't get it, inflation can't touch it, the gnawing tooth of time and the foul breath of decay can't destroy it. It's there; that's your inheritance, but the next verse says, "For you, who are kept by the power of God." You're kept by the power of God. It's not a matter of your holding onto Him; it's a matter of Him holding onto you.

People say, "Just pray for me that I'll hold out faithful to the end." Well, we should pray for one another that we'll be faithful Christians, but it's not our holding out, it's Him holding us. Jesus said, "Neither shall anyone snatch them out of My hand. My Father, who has given them to Me, is greater than all; and no one is able to snatch them out of My Father's hand" (John 10:28–29).

Can you imagine a power that is strong enough to pry open the hand of God and take you out? Some people say, "I think the devil could take you away from God." Oh, you do? You think the devil can take you away? Well, then, if he could, why hasn't he? Think about it. Hasn't the devil been nice to you? He has the power, but he just hasn't done it. Now that's a strange doctrine, isn't it? You're going to heaven by the goodness of the devil. No, no, no! You're going to heaven by the grace of God, and the only reason the devil hasn't taken you out of the hand of God is he can't.

"My sheep hear My voice, and I know them, and they follow Me. And I give them eternal life, and ... [no one is able to] snatch them out of My hand" (John 10:27–29). Friend, we're kept by the power of God.

Don't ever get the idea that because you're eternally secure, it makes no difference how you live. God will cure that theory in a hurry because God will carry you to the woodshed. "For whom the LORD loves He chastens" (Heb. 12:6). Don't get the idea this is a license to sin—that's foolish.

I Sin All I Want To

Some people say, "If I believe in eternal security, I can just get saved and sin all I want to." I sin all I want to. I sin *more* than I want to. I don't want to. Nothing would please me better than to know I'd never sin again. One of these days, when God is finished with me, I will never sin again, but I'd just as soon eat dirt as to willingly sin. And if you still want to, you need to get your "wanter" fixed; you need to be born again. "If any one is in Christ, he is a new creation; old things have passed away; behold all things have become new."

I've given you eight reasons, straight from the Bible, that you can know that you are eternally secure. Remember, it's great to be saved. It's even better to be saved and know you're saved. And it is even more wonderful that you can be saved, know that you are saved, and know that you can never lose it.

STUDY QUESTIONS

1. What would be changed in your approach to the average day if you were totally confident in the sufficiency of your salvation in Christ? Why would your human nature see this as an escape clause from responsibility?

2. Why do you think God conceived a plan by which human beings could be forgiven of their sins and promised eternity with Him without requiring any effort on their part? How does your answer to this question magnify the truth of your eternal security in Christ?

3. What evidence could you present from your own life to confirm the inefficiency of good deeds and good intentions in making you blameless before God? How do you still, even in subtle attempts, try to earn or manipulate your way into God's good graces?

4. Knowing the power of God as evidenced in Scripture and taught by the Lord Jesus, what could possibly be strong enough to prevent Him from accomplishing His plans for your life? What kind of havoc could this confidence wreak on all your fretting and worrying?

5. What is the value of these intervening years between your salvation experience with Christ and your ultimate entrance into glory? Why the necessity for struggle, turmoil, pain, and loss if your righteous position before God has already been established?

6. At what level does the biblical portrait of Christ praying for His disciples touch you? Knowing that Christ has best-for-you expectations, how can you keep yourself and your stubborn will reminded of His intercessory role for you?

7. In addition to His prayers for you, how have you also experienced His attentive love in the form of discipline and chastisement? Why would He bother with such corrective measures if He didn't have plans for you on the other side of your disobedience?

4

Every Christian Ought to Know
How to Pray (with Power)

In this manner, therefore, pray: Our Father in heaven, Hallowed be Your name. Your kingdom come. Your will be done on earth as it is in heaven. Give us this day our daily bread. And forgive us our debts, as we forgive our debtors. And do not lead us into temptation, but deliver us from the evil one. For Yours is the kingdom and the power and the glory forever. Amen.

MATTHEW 6:9–13

Praying with power! There's not a more important subject in all the world for a Christian than to learn how to pray. Not only to learn *how* to pray but to pray *with power,* to pray in the Spirit, to pray to get prayers answered. As Christians we must realize that nothing lies beyond the reach of prayer except that which lies outside the will of God. Prayer can do anything that God can do, and God can do anything!

In Matthew 6:9–13, our Lord shows us how to pray. Notice, He did not say, "Pray this prayer." He said, "In this manner, therefore, pray." This is not a prayer simply to be repeated mindlessly. Sometimes at a gathering in a civic auditorium, someone may say, "Now let's just all stand and say the Lord's Prayer." This is not necessarily appropriate.

In the first place, many of these people may not even be Christians, and they have no real right, as we're going to see in a moment, to call God their Father. Second, we do not just stand and say a prayer. Prayers are not meant to be said; they are meant to be prayed. You might ask, "What's the difference?"

Suppose I were to come to your house and sit in your living room, and you said to me, "Say a conversation." That would be silly. Prayer is talking with God, not merely repeating words. Jesus said we are not to pray with vain repetition. The key is in Matthew 6:9, "In this manner, therefore, pray." This is a guide to show us how to pray. Pray like *this!*

I confess there may be times when the words of this prayer fit my need perfectly. Then I may want to repeat word for word what our Lord taught here. But I am not merely repeating words; I am praying out of my heart to our great God using *His* words.

Learning How to Pray

For many Christians the major failure in life is failing to learn to pray. There is no sin in your life that proper prayer could not avoid. There is no need in your life that proper prayer could not supply that need. That is why I emphasize that nothing lies outside the reach of prayer except that which lies outside the will of God. What fools we are if we do not learn to pray!

It is important that we look at the model prayer in Matthew 6:9–13 that our Lord gave us. Here He tells us how to pray.

The Persons of Prayer

Look in Matthew 6:9 which says, "In this manner, therefore, pray: Our Father in heaven, Hallowed be Your name."

Who are the persons in this prayer? A child and his Father. We're coming to God and speaking to God, as our Father. It is important to understand this because real, powerful prayer—prayer that prevails—is for the children of God.

You might say that this is to be taken for granted because everybody is a child of God. No, they're not! *Not* everyone *is a child of God.* Jesus said to the unsaved Pharisees, "You are of your father the devil, and the desires of your father you want to do" (John 8:44).

Who are the true children of God? The Bible says in the first chapter of John, concerning the Lord Jesus, "But as many as received Him, to them He gave the right to become children of God, to those who believe in His name" (1:12). So not everybody is a child of God—only believers!

The Children of God

Often we hear people speak of the universal fatherhood of God and the universal brotherhood of man. That is not right.

God is not universally the Father of all, and all people are not necessarily brothers. We may be brothers in our humanity, but spiritually we are not brothers until we are born into the family of God and have one common Father. God becomes our Father when we are born into the family of God.

Some may argue that since God created us that He is the Father of us. Well, God also created rats, roaches, buzzards, and rattlesnakes. He's not their Father! No, He does not become the Father by creation; He *becomes the Father* by new birth.

The first thing that must occur if you want your prayers to be answered and you want your prayers to be powerful is to become a child of God. In order to be a child of God, you must receive the Lord Jesus Christ as your personal Savior. Have you done that? Does Christ live in your heart? If so, then you are ready to pray.

When you can say, "Father," you'll see how easy it is to pray.

Sometimes I have asked people to pray, and they say, "Oh, I'm sorry, I can't pray." And these people are professing Christians! Why can't they pray? Surely they can talk to an earthly father. Anyone who can talk to an earthly father can talk to their heavenly Father. You do not have to be an amateur Shakespeare in order to pray. You do not have to pray in old English, or convoluted terms, or poetic meter. You can just talk to God out of your heart. That's the way a child talks to his father.

Suppose, when my children were living at home, my daughter came to me and said, "Hail thou eminent pastor of Bellevue Baptist Church. I welcome thee home from thy sojourn. Wouldest thou grant to thy second daughter Janice some money that I may sojourn to yonder apothecary and procure for myself some cosmetics to adorn my face?" That would have been ridiculous, wouldn't it?

This is the scenario that would more likely have happened: "Daddy, I love you. It's so good to have you home. Daddy, I need some money. I need to get some things at the drugstore." She would have spoken to me out of her heart because I am her father. Now that doesn't mean that she would be disrespectful to me. It does not mean that we are to be irreverent to God either. We can speak to God right out of our hearts and say to Him, "Father."

Galatians 4:6 says, "And because you are sons, God has sent forth the Spirit of His Son into your hearts, crying out, 'Abba, Father.'" The word *Abba* is an Aramaic word, a diminutive term. The best translation is "Daddy."

Have you ever thought about calling the great God—the One who scooped out the seas and heaped up the mountains and flung out the stars, who runs this mighty universe—have you ever thought about calling Him, "Daddy"? Would that be irreverent? No.

God's Spirit in our hearts cries out "Abba, Father" if you have been born into the family of God. If you have been born into the family of God, you can spiritually crawl up into His lap, put your arms around His neck, and talk to Him, as you would to your own father.

Some people think they have to pray through a priest or a saint. They illustrate this by using the example of talking to the president. They say you would not go directly to the president; you would go to your senator or congressman. Then he would go to the president for you. They surmise from this scenario that you cannot go directly to God, but you can go to the priest or saint who then goes to God for you.

Well, my friend, I am not going to go through my congressman if the president is my daddy. If the president is my own dear father, I'm not going to say, "Mr. Congressman, will you tell Dad something for me?" Not if the president is my father.

You can go directly to God, your Father, if you are born again by faith in the Lord Jesus Christ as your personal Savior and Lord.

The Purpose of Prayer

Matthew 6:10 says, "Your kingdom come. Your will be done on earth as it is in heaven." Prayer has one purpose and one purpose only. And that is that God's will be done.

Prayer is not an exercise where we bend God's will and make it fit our will. Too many people have the notion that prayer is talking God into doing something that He ordinarily would not want to do. This is not true. Prayer is seeking the will of God and following it. Prayer is the way of getting God's will done on earth.

Some say, "I knew there must be some catch to it. All I get to have is the will of God. I don't want it if I don't get what I want." If you're thinking this way, let me tell you that God wants for you what you would want for yourself if you had enough sense to want it. God's will is *best* for you. God's will is not something that you *have* to do. God's will is something that you *get* to do.

God loves you so much. All good things will He give to those who walk uprightly in Him. God longs to bless you. God yearns to bless you. You must come to the place where you can know the will of God. Successful prayer is finding the will of God and getting in on it. You are not *hemmed in* by the will of God; you are *freed up* by the will of God.

The Bible says, "Now this is the confidence that we have in Him, that if we ask anything according to His will, He hears us" (1 John 5:14). We must pray according to the will of God. But what is His will?

Some things are plainly stated in the Scriptures as God's will. For instance, the Bible says that the Lord is "not willing that any should perish" (2 Pet. 3:9). Obviously when a person is saved, God desires that sanctification because the Bible says, "This is the will of God, your sanctification" (1 Thess. 4:3).

While we know that certain things are the will of God, in other matters we must seek His will. Should you move to another city to take that new job? Should you sell your home? Should you go to this college or that college? Should you marry this boy or that girl? In all matters, if we seek the will of God, we will come to know the will of God.

How can we know the will of God? Jesus said, "If you abide in Me, and My words abide in you, you will ask what you desire, and it shall be done for you" (John 15:7). Now notice He says, "If you abide in Me, and My words abide in you." To "abide" is to lean upon Jesus moment by moment—to look to Jesus and depend upon Jesus. It also means that we are to read the Word of God daily, allowing it to move from the written pages into our hearts. Then the Holy Spirit shows us *how* to pray and *what* to pray. This is what the Bible calls praying in the Spirit.

The Holy Spirit in us helps us to pray. We pray *to* the Father, *through* the Son, and *in* the Spirit. If we surrender to the Spirit of

God and abide in Christ, then His Word abides in us. Therefore, we can pray for whatever we will. Because strangely and wonderfully, what we now will is what He wills because we now have the mind of Christ. As we pray, we think the thoughts of Christ after Him.

One of the sweetest lessons I ever learned about prayer is this: *the prayer that gets to heaven is the prayer that starts in heaven.* What we do is just close the circuit. God lays something upon our hearts to pray for, we pray for it, and it goes right back to heaven.

Prayer is the Holy Spirit finding a desire in the heart of the Father and then putting that desire into our hearts and then sending it back to heaven in the power of the cross. Isn't that beautiful! And so what is the purpose of prayer? "Your kingdom come. Your will be done." We are to seek the will of God in all of our praying. That does not mean fewer blessings for us; it means more blessings.

The Provision of Prayer

Matthew 6:11 says, "Give us this day our daily bread." The Lord is telling us that in a practical way He will provide for our needs. One of the greatest verses in all of the Bible is, "My God shall supply all your need according to His riches in glory by Christ Jesus" (Phil. 4:19).

It does not say, "My God shall supply all your wants," because there are times when we want things we do not need. There are also times when we need things we don't want. My dad used to say, "You need a spanking." He was right. I *needed* one, but I didn't *want* one.

God will supply all of our needs and more according to His riches. It does not say *out* of His riches. A millionaire may give you ten dollars out of his riches, but that's not necessarily *according to* his riches. But my God shall supply all of our needs according to His riches in glory by Christ Jesus. We can come and say, "Father, give me today my daily bread."

This verse does not imply that all we can ask for is bread. We have many needs. That's the reason I was careful to point out to you at the beginning that this is not a prayer to be mechanically repeated. It is a model prayer. Jesus did not say, "Pray this prayer." He said, "Pray in this manner."

If you need bread, ask God for a loaf. If you need a job, ask Him for a job. If you need a house, ask Him for a house. Let the Holy Spirit show you what to ask for and then pray in the Spirit that your needs are met. I am convinced that many Christians do not have their needs met—when God desires to meet those needs—because they cheat themselves by failing to pray.

In James 4:2, we read that "you do not have because you do not ask."

When I was in college, I pastored a little country church on the Atlantic side of Florida, near the Indian River. It's a beautiful spot where some of the best citrus fruit in all of the world grows. When I was getting ready to return to college, I went down there and ran into one of the deacons. He had two big canvas bags filled with oranges, grapefruit, and tangerines. He said, "Adrian, this is for you." I said, "I can't eat all those oranges; they'll spoil." He said, "Take them back to college and give them away."

I put them in the trunk of my car, drove back to college, and put them in a closet. A day or two later, I was eating lunch and looking in the backyard when I saw a little boy sneaking around. He never knew I was watching him, so I decided that I would see what he was up to.

I saw he was going to steal an orange from a tree in my backyard. The orange tree was what we call a sour orange tree—an ornamental fruit, not meant to be eaten. He plucked one and ran away. I didn't have any extra money in those days, but I really believe I would have given a dollar to see this little boy take the first bite of that bitter orange.

But here is the irony of this example. Had that little fellow just come and knocked on my door and said, "Mister, may I have one of those oranges?" I would have said, "No son, you cannot. But if you'll come up here, I'll load you down with oranges." I had oranges that I was longing to give. That is what the Bible means by "we have not because we ask not."

One of these days when we are up in heaven, the Lord may take us by a great big closet, open the door, and say, "Look in there. You see all those things? Those were yours. They are provisions I made for you, but you wanted the devil's sour oranges, and that's what you got." You had not because you asked not.

This is the provision of the prayer: "Give us this day our daily bread."

The Pardon of Prayer

Matthew 6:12 says, "And forgive us our debts, as we forgive our debtors."

- Sometimes prayer is not answered because we are not praying to God as a Father. We have never been saved.

- Sometimes prayer is not answered because we are not praying in the will of God. We're not saying, "Your kingdom come, Your will be done." Instead, we're saying, "My kingdom come and my will be done."

- Sometimes our prayers are not answered because they are not asked. We simply do not say, "Father, give me what I need."

- And then sometimes our prayers are not answered because there is unconfessed, unrepented sin in our lives.

Along with asking for what we need, we need to remember that one thing we may need is forgiveness. That is why our Lord taught us to pray, "And forgive us our debts as we forgive our debtors."

I want to give you two prayer promises. Here is the first one. "If I regard iniquity in my heart, the Lord will not hear" (Ps. 66:18). And the second is, "Behold the LORD's hand is not shortened, that it cannot save; nor His ear heavy, that it cannot hear. But your iniquities have separated you from your God; and your sins have hidden His face from you, so that He will not hear" (Isa. 59:1–2). Not that He *cannot* hear; it is that sin has come between you and a Holy God. If we regard iniquity in our hearts, the Lord will not hear us.

Scripture does not say if you have sinned the Lord will not hear you. If that were the case, He would not hear any of us. Because we know what the Word of God tells us about ourselves,

"For all have sinned and fall short of the glory of God" (Rom. 3:23). And, "If we say that we have no sin, we deceive ourselves, and the truth is not in us" (1 John 1:8). God tells us that if we regard iniquity in our hearts then He will not hear us. What does that mean?

Let's suppose you are like the average Christian and say, "Nobody's perfect. Everybody has some sin in his life, so this one is mine." You have a little pet sin. It may be a grudge, an attitude, or a habit. There is no repentance and sorrow for that sin but rather a regard for it.

Now let's say that you come to God to pray. And you say, "Lord, You know my child is sick, and I want You to heal my child." Do you think God's going to hear your prayer? No, He will not hear your prayer! You see it's not merely that you have sinned but that you have regard for that sin. And if He did what you were asking of Him, He would be encouraging you to sin. So He will not do what you ask. You must deal with your sin first. You must repent of it. You must get that sin out of your heart, out of your life. And the only way to get it out is to come to the Lord and ask His forgiveness.

The Bible says in 1 John 1:9, "If we confess our sins, He is faithful and just to forgive us our sins and to cleanse us from all unrighteousness." If you are praying with unrepented sin in your heart and life, you're wasting your breath! Your prayers are not getting any higher than the lightbulbs.

Also remember that God forgives us in the manner that we forgive others. How do you forgive those who sin against you? You say, "I'm not going to forgive her." God says, "I'm not going to forgive you." Then you say, "OK, if it's that way, I'll forgive her, but I won't have any more to do with her." God says, "OK, I'll forgive you and never have any more to do with you."

Now you see, we are praying with conditions. We're saying, "Lord, You forgive me in the same manner I forgive others."

I heard about a little girl who was angry with her mother. Early one night, her mother put her to bed and told her to say her prayers before she went to sleep. The little girl got down on her knees and prayed for her brothers, sisters, daddy, aunts, uncles, and everything. Then she finished and said, "Amen." She looked up at her mother and said, "I guess you noticed you weren't in it." Well, that kind of prayer is not the kind of prayer that gets answered.

Is there unconfessed sin in your heart right now? It may be big, it may be small, but if there is sin in your life, then don't be amazed that God is not hearing your prayer. The Bible teaches in Psalm 66:18, "If I regard iniquity in my heart, the Lord will not hear."

The Protection of Prayer

Now that brings us to another important aspect of prayer—the *protection* of prayer. Matthew 6:13 says, "And do not lead us into temptation, but deliver us from the evil one." There is a devil. He is very real, and he wants to keep you from praying. He says to his demons, "Keep that person from praying because if you can keep him from praying we can beat him every time. But if he prays, he will beat us every time!"

It has been said that the devil trembles when he sees even the weakest saint upon his knees. And so, my friend, we need to pray. "Lord, lead us not into temptation."

And that brings up a real question. Does God tempt us? James 1:13 says that God tempts no man with evil. Second Peter 2:9 also says He "knows how to deliver the godly out of temptations." So this passage of the Lord's Prayer may be translated, "Lead us lest we fall into temptation." We need to pray daily that the Lord will deliver us.

Let me ask you a question. Have you ever committed a sin, asked God to forgive you, and He did? Now let me ask you another question. After you asked God to forgive you for that sin, did you commit that same sin or one like it again—even after God forgave you? And have you ever repeated that sin as many as ten times and come to God and said, "It's me again; I did it again"?

Does He continue to forgive us? If we're sincere, He does absolutely. "Seventy times seven" He will forgive you. As many times as you sin He will forgive! Praise His sweet name!

As far as God is concerned, it is the first time you ever sinned! Because He not only forgives, but He forgets our sins too! "As far as the east is from the west, so far has He removed our transgression from us" (Ps. 103:12). And in Hebrews 8:12, God tells us that He will remember our lawless deeds no more.

But wait a minute! Don't you get tired of coming back with the same old sins? Aren't you embarrassed? And aren't you ashamed that you come back and say, "Lord, it's me again. I did it again. I failed again. God have mercy on me"? Why do you keep on coming, as in Matthew 6:12, and say, "Forgive me my trespasses"?

I think it is because you have understood verse 12 but you have not understood verse 13.

Verse 12 is the *pardon* of the prayer, but verse 13 is the *protection* of the prayer. And the reason we have to come back to God so many times and ask His forgiveness is that we have not put on the protection of prayer that would keep us from repeatedly falling into temptation.

Many of us jump out of bed in the morning feeling pretty good, and we do not sense any real need for prayer. The sun is shining. We have our breakfast, a cup of coffee, and sail out of the house feeling fine. And then sometime during the day the unexpected happens. We have a head-on collision with Satan. Satan digs a pit for your feet every day. He knows how to ensnare you.

The devil is not all that interested in you as a person. His real war is with God. Evil people have always known if they cannot harm someone directly, they will try to harm someone the person loves. And that is why the devil wants to harm you—so he can get at God indirectly.

And so we have become pawns in this war. The devil is the real enemy! He has made plans to sabotage us and harm our loved ones. But we go sailing through the day. Everything's fine. Then Satan tosses a bombshell in our lap. It comes so unexpectedly and we fail. At the end of the day, we say, "God, I'm so sorry! Lord, forgive me!" And He does.

But this is not a prayer to be prayed at the *end* of the day. This is a prayer to be prayed at the *beginning* of the day. This prayer is not the latch that closes the door at the end of the day. It is the key that opens the door at the beginning of the day.

As we wake up, we must put on the armor of our Lord Jesus Christ and make no provision for the flesh. We must immerse ourselves in the presence and power of God.

God builds a wall of fire about us as we say, "Dear Lord, deliver us from the evil one. Dear Lord, lead us lest we fall into temptation." How important that we learn how to pray!

We don't pray for protection because we think we are capable of handling it. The worst thing is not our prayerlessness; it is our pride! We think that we can go through the day and overcome the devil with our own strength. The best protection is to get off the defensive and get on the offensive.

I have a friend who was a linebacker for the Miami Dolphins. They called him Captain Crunch. He was tough and big, *and* he loved the Lord. I heard him talk about a conversation he had with his coach one day. His coach asked him, "Mike, will you do some scouting for me?" And Mike responded, "Sure, Coach, what kind of players you looking for?" The coach said, "Well, there is the player who gets knocked down and just stays there." Mike said, "We don't want him do we, Coach?" The coach said, "No!" Then the coach said, "Then there's the guy you knock down and he gets up. You knock him down again and he gets up. And you knock him down, and he just keeps getting up." Mike said, "That's the guy we want, isn't it, Coach?" The coach said, "No, we don't. I want you to find that guy that's knocking everybody down. Now that's the guy I want!"

I thank God that every time we get knocked down, He picks us up. But wouldn't you like to resist the devil and make him flee from you rather than just saying, "Lord, I'm down again, pick me up"? The Bible says in Romans 12:21, "Do not be overcome by evil, but overcome evil with good." We need to get off the defensive and on the offensive by praying, "Dear Lord, deliver me from the evil one, and lead me lest I fall into temptation."

The Praise of Prayer

Now the last thing I want you to notice is the *praise* of prayer in Matthew 6:13, "For Yours is the kingdom and the power and the glory for ever. Amen." It ends on a note of praise. And it begins on a note of praise: "Our Father in heaven, hallowed be Your name."

All powerful prayer is prayer that is packed with praise. Why? Because praise is an expression of faith! Prayer is faith turned inside out. *Faith* causes our prayers to be answered.

When we pray in the will of God with clean hearts, then we have every right to expect God to answer us. So we can begin to praise Him. And if we are having difficulty in our praying, it might be because we are not praising enough.

Billy Sunday said we need to pull some of the groans out of our prayers and shove in a few hallelujahs! Praise is a wonderful, powerful thing.

Petition goes into God's presence to carry something away. But praise goes into God's presence to stay there forever. It pleases the Lord. It blesses the Lord when we offer Him the sacrifice of praise. Powerful prayer is crammed full of praise. God inhabits the praises of His people (see Ps. 22:3).

When I got ready to go away to college, my dad said, "Son, I would like to pay your way to college; I'm not able to, but I would like to." And I said, "Dad, I appreciate the fact that you want to."

God called me to preach, and He has taken care of me. I lived from hand to mouth, and often it was God's hand to my mouth. But it meant so much to me when my dad said, "Son, I would like to if I could."

My heavenly Father will never say to me, "Son, I would like to but I can't." My heavenly Father is the King of kings. We have the heart of the Father and the hand of the King!

We have a Father who can *hear* us, and we have the King who can *answer* us. We should pray earnestly, fervently, expectantly, and praisefully unto Him.

I was talking to a young boy, and he said, "God has called me to preach, and He wants me to go to school, but I don't have any money. So I don't guess I can go." I said, "If I could get a millionaire to help you, would you go?" His eyes lit up, and he said, "I sure would." I said, "Well, you have the One who owns the world— Almighty God."

Where God *guides* He *provides*. If God can't do it, who can? God may use a millionaire, or He may use some other means, but I want to tell you that His is the kingdom, the power, and the glory! What a great God we have to pray to! And what fools we are if we do not learn how to pray.

You do not have a failure in your life except that which is really a prayer failure. There is not a sin in your life that proper prayer would not have avoided. There is not a need in your life that could not be met if you learned to pray. So I want you to say with the disciples, and with my own heart:

Lord, teach me to pray!

STUDY QUESTIONS

1. How would you define or describe your current, personal experience with prayer? What would you say is missing from it? What do you wish your prayer life was more like, and why do you think you haven't reached this level of intimacy and faith in relating with God?

2. How did your earthly father exemplify many of the tender, engaged qualities of God as Father, and how is that a blessing to you in prayer? Or what obstacles do you perhaps bring into prayer from your past experiences, struggling to interact with Him in such close relationship?

3. What have you prayed for recently that you have not yet received? How do you try to discern whether your prayer is in the will of God? What might He be trying to achieve in you by either withholding or delaying the answer that you desire?

4. What would help you make prayer more of an unceasing activity in your life (1 Thess. 5:17), rather than just an obligatory act to be performed at set times and places—in the morning, during church services, at the dinner hour?

5. Try to imagine life without prayer. What would be different if God had not chosen to give us this avenue of access to Him, despite how invisible and mysterious it can often seem? How does

seeing prayer as a privilege rather than a compulsion affect its enjoyment to you?

6. Why is it understandable that the lack of forgiveness in your heart toward another person also creates a barrier between you and God in prayer? What specific, known issue of unforgiveness still exists in your life that needs to be gotten out of the way?

7. If you had to measure the percentages of your prayer life, how large a portion would you say is taken up with worship? With intercession for others? With yourself and your own needs? What do these admissions tell you about your motivations and understanding of prayer?

5

Every Christian Ought to Know
How to Understand the Bible

---

*Open my eyes, that I may see wondrous
things from Your law.*

PSALM 119:18

A wise man once said, "These hath God married and no man shall part, dust on the Bible and drought in the heart." If you do not know, love, understand, practice, and obey the Word of God, I can tell you without stutter, stammer, or apology that you are not a victorious Christian.

As you read this chapter, I want you to learn how to study your Bible, how to make it burst aflame in your hand. Knowledge is power. That's true in any realm, whether it's business, athletics, or theology. I want us to look at how to obtain knowledge from the Word of God.

People today need truth. Someone in Kenya once wrote this prayer: "Lord, from the cowardice that dares not face new truth, from the laziness that is contented with half-truth, from the arrogance which thinks it has all truth, good Lord, deliver me. Amen."

I hope that you'll not have cowardice and be afraid of truth, that you'll not have laziness and accept half-truth, or that you'll not have arrogance and think that you need no truth. It is knowledge, it is truth, that transforms.

A business sign read, "We are not what we think we are; what we think, we are." Did you understand that? You are what you think. The Bible says in Proverbs 23:7, "For as he thinks in his heart, so is he."

If that is true and if knowledge is power, we need the knowledge of the Word of God to have spiritual power. We need to be molded, motivated, and managed by the Word of God. And yet for many people, the Bible remains a closed book, a mysterious book. They really do not understand it.

There is no cheap way, no lazy way, no magical way to understand the Bible. But it is not impossible. As a matter of fact, it is joyful and thrilling.

Psalm 119 is by far the longest psalm in the Bible. The writer of this psalm gives us a number of statements about the Word of God. In fact, the entire psalm, well over one hundred verses, is dealing with the Word of God, to help us know and understand the Word of God.

As you read this chapter, I want you to take note of three things. If you'll do these three things, the Bible will burst aflame in your heart, in your mind, and in your life:

- Appreciate the *virtues* of the Word of God.
- Assimilate the *vitality* of the Word of God.
- Appropriate the *values* of the Word of God.

Appreciate the Virtues of the Word of God

If you don't appreciate the virtues of the Word of God, you're not going to have any desire to learn His Word or know it. Many people do not understand the great value and virtue of the Word of God. You must appreciate the Word of God.

The Bible Is Timeless

Psalm 119:89 says, "Forever, O LORD, Your word is settled in heaven."

The Bible is not the book of the month or even the book of the year. The Bible is the book of the ages. It is an unchanging, timeless book.

Psalm 119:152 says, "Concerning Your testimonies, I have known of old that You have founded them forever."

Forever! God says that it is done. It is settled in heaven. Psalm 119:160 says, "The entirety of Your word is truth, and every one of Your righteous judgments endures forever."

Other books come and go. The Bible is here to stay. Thousands of years have passed since the Bible was written. Empires have risen and fallen. Civilizations have come and gone. Science has pushed back the frontiers of knowledge. And yet the Bible stands.

Emperors have decreed the extermination of the Bible, and atheists have railed against the Bible. Agnostics have cynically sneered at the Bible, and liberals have moved heaven and earth to remove the miracles from the Bible. Materialists have simply ignored the Bible, but the Bible stands. The Bible is settled in heaven.

The late, great Dr. Robert G. Lee had this to say about the Bible: "All of its enemies have not torn one hole in its holy vesture, nor stolen one flower from its wonderful garden, nor diluted one drop of honey from its abundant hive, nor broken one string on its thousand-stringed harp, nor drowned one sweet word in infidel ink."

Dr. Lee was simply saying what God says about Himself: "Forever, O Lord, Your word is settled in heaven" (Ps. 119:89). In the New Testament, 1 Peter 1:25 says, "But the word of the Lord endures forever."

The Bible is timeless, ultimate, indestructible.

The Bible Is Truthful

Psalm 119:142 says, "Your righteousness is an everlasting righteousness, and Your law is truth." Verse 151 says, "You are near, O Lord, and all Your commandments are truth." Then verse 160 says, "The entirety of Your word is truth."

In the Gospel of John, Pilate asked Jesus, "What is truth?" (John 18:38). Jesus had already answered that question in John 17:17 when, speaking to the Father, He said, "Your word is truth." In a world that has lost its appreciation for truth, you can say without stutter or stammer that the Bible is truth.

Today there are all kinds of attacks on the truth of the Bible. There's the frontal attack of liberals who deny the truth of the Bible. But there's also an attack from the rear, which is perhaps more insidious. These are not the people who deny the truth of the Bible. These are the people who put their own experience over the Word of God. They say, "I know what I feel or what I think." Sometimes, they'll even argue and say, "I don't care what the Bible says. Let me tell you what I experienced."

Paul had to deal with some of those people in Corinth. He said to them in 1 Corinthians 14:37–38: "If anyone thinks himself to be a prophet or spiritual, let him acknowledge that the things which I write to you are the commandments of the Lord."

Apparently some people in Corinth ventured into charismatic hocus-pocus and went wild about tongues, prophecies, visions, and ecstasies. Paul tried to set them in order, but they said, "Let me tell you, Brother Paul, what a spiritual man I am. And, let me tell you, Brother Paul, I have the gift of prophecy."

Paul says, "If you think you're a prophet or if you think you're spiritual, then you will acknowledge what I say is the Word of God." He goes on to say in verse 38, "But if anyone is ignorant, let him be ignorant."

There is the frontal attack against the truth of the Bible by those who rail against it and deny it. There's an attack from the rear by those who want to substitute their own experience for the Word of God. And there's an attack from the flank. These people don't necessarily deny the Bible. But they want to replace it or prop it up with psychology and with philosophy and other things, as if the Bible itself is not good enough.

Friend, the Bible is true, and if you're looking for truth, you can find it in the Bible.

Why? Second Timothy 3:16 says, "All Scripture is given by inspiration of God." That word *inspiration* is used only once in the Bible, but what a magnificent word it is. In Greek the word is *theopneustos*. The word literally means "God-breathed." *Theo* means God. *Pneustos* means breathed. The Bible says that all Scripture is the breath of God. It is God-breathed.

In Matthew 4:4, Jesus said, "Man shall not live by bread alone, but by every word that proceeds from the mouth of God." Jesus was talking about the Bible. He said that every word proceeds from the mouth of God. It is not simply that God breathed into the Scriptures. God breathed the Scriptures out. Yes, He used men such as Isaiah, Jeremiah, Matthew, Mark, and Paul. But these men held the pen of God. They were the voice of God as God was speaking. The Bible is true because the God of truth cannot speak error.

If you read the Old Testament, you will find phrases like "the Word of the Lord" or "the Word of God" or "God spoke" or "the Lord said" used 3,808 times. If the Bible is not the Word of God, it's the biggest bundle of lies that has ever come to planet Earth. The Bible is truth, absolutely.

The Bible Is Treasured

Because the Bible is a *timeless* book and a *truthful* book, it should therefore be a *treasured* book. In Psalm 119:72, the psalmist says, "The law of Your mouth is better to me than thousands of coins of gold and silver."

Is that true of you? God knows that it is absolutely true of me. If you were to ask me to choose between a huge stack of gold, silver, rubies, diamonds, stocks, and bonds on the one hand, or the Word of God on the other, I would not hesitate. I would choose the Word of God. Psalm 119:103 says, "How sweet are Your words to my taste, sweeter than honey to my mouth!" Verse 127 says, "Therefore I love Your commandments more than gold, yes, than fine gold."

The Bible is to be a treasured book. The saints and the heroes of our faith have pillowed their heads on the Word of God as they walked through the chilly waters of the river of death. The martyrs who died for the witness of Jesus Christ have held the Bible to their bosoms as the creeping flames came around their feet. The members of the early church loved the Word of God. They never questioned it, and they argued little about it. They preached it, proclaimed it, pronounced it, and poured it forth like white-hot lava. They loved it, lived it, practiced it, trusted it, and obeyed it. They claimed it constantly.

Do you know why the Bible is treasured? You've known it for a long time. "Jesus loves me, this I know, for the Bible tells me so." That's it. "Jesus loves me, this I know, for the Bible tells me so." You will never have a victorious Christian life if you do not love this book.

The Bible is like treasure. Suppose there was buried treasure in your backyard. You'd go down to the hardware store and get a spade if you didn't already have one. The Bible is God's treasure book. It is a timeless book. It is a truthful book. Therefore, you must appreciate the virtues of the Word of God. If you don't appreciate the virtues of the Word of God, you're not going to have any desire to understand it.

Assimilate the Vitality of the Word of God

The word *vitality* means "alive." The Bible is a *living* book. Hebrews 4:12 says, "For the word of God is living and powerful." The word *powerful* comes from the Greek word *energes* which means "effective." This is the word from which we get our word *energy.* The Bible is alive. It is effective.

In John 6:63, Jesus spoke to a group of unbelievers and His disciples saying, "The words that I speak to you are spirit, and they are life." The Bible pulsates with life. For instance, you don't just read a cookbook. You use its instructions to prepare a meal, then you eat it. If you don't assimilate it, no matter how much you appreciate it, what good is it going to do you?

Pray over the Word of God

How do you assimilate the Word of God? Pray over it. Psalm 119:12 says, "Blessed are You, O LORD! Teach me Your statutes." Have you ever prayed that? "Lord God, be my Teacher." Pray over the Word of God and ask God to teach you.

First, *your eyes will be opened.* Read in Psalm 119:18: "Open my eyes, that I may see wondrous things from Your law." God will open your eyes. You may have 20/20 vision, but God has to open your eyes in order for you to behold the wondrous things in His Word.

After His resurrection, Jesus walked with two disciples on the road to Emmaus. The Bible says that He began to talk to them about the Old Testament, the Law, and the Prophets. Then, Luke 24:45 says, "And He opened their understanding, that they might comprehend the Scriptures." Wouldn't you like God to do that for you?

When you pray over the Word of God, not only will your eyes be opened, but *your heart will be stirred*. Psalm 119:36 says, "Incline my heart to Your testimonies, and not to covetousness." If you don't have a desire for the Word of God, then pray, "Oh God, please incline my heart. Move my heart, open my eyes, stir my heart."

And then, when your eyes are opened and your heart is stirred, *your mind is going to be enlightened*. Psalm 119:73 says, "Your hands have made me and fashioned me; give me understanding, that I may learn Your commandments."

How often in sermon preparation have I put down my pencil and bowed my head to say, "Oh my God, help me to understand this. God, give me understanding." When we pray, our eyes are opened, our hearts are moved, and our minds are enlightened to understand the Word of God.

Ponder the Word of God

Psalm 119:15 says, "I will meditate on Your precepts." Verse 147 of this psalm says, "I rise before the dawning of the morning, and cry for help; I hope in Your word." In other words, he had a quiet time. The psalmist continues in verse 148: "My eyes are awake through the night watches, that I may meditate on Your word."

It takes time to ponder the Word of God. If you have to rise an hour early, do it. If you have to stay up an hour late, do it. Do whatever it takes so that you might ponder the Word of God. And may I suggest that as you ponder the Word of God, you keep a pad and pencil handy? I always read the Bible with a pen or a pencil in my hand. Why? Because I'm *expecting to receive something.* If you're not doing that, it tells me that you're not expecting to receive anything.

If you're expecting to receive something, you should be ready to write it down. You say, "I'll remember it." I hope you do. But the weakest ink is better than the best memory. It's such a simple thing to get a pad and pencil when you open the Bible. You pray over it, you ponder it, and then you get ready for God to speak to you.

And when you read the Bible, use your sanctified common sense. Don't just jump into the middle of a chapter or the middle of a book somewhere with no plan. The Bible is like any other book in that it contains a number of different forms of speech. You see poetry as poetry. You see prophecy as prophecy. You see precept as precept. You see promise as promise. You see proverb as proverb.

If you try to turn the proverbs into promises, you'll lose your religion. The proverbs are not promises. They're proverbs. What is a proverb? A proverb is a general principle that when generally applied brings a general result.

For example, the book of Proverbs has ways to be healthy, wealthy, and wise. But you can do all those things and get hit by a truck. You're not very healthy anymore. And you're certainly not wealthy; you left it all. If you'd been wise, you would've looked both ways. The proverbs are good, but don't try to turn the proverbs into promises.

Look at the Bible and consider what you are reading. Ask yourself, "Is this a precept? Is this a prophecy? Is this poetry? Is this prose? Is this proverb? Is this promise?" God gave you a mind. But God doesn't zap you with knowledge. You have the mind of Christ. Use your mind. As you study the Bible, you should ponder it.

Sometimes people ask, "Is the Bible to be interpreted literally or figuratively?" The answer is, "Yes." The Bible is to be interpreted figuratively *and* literally all at the same time.

The Bible, for example, is full of symbols. In the book of Revelation, the devil is symbolized as a huge dragon. He has a tail so long that he sweeps a third of the stars from heaven.

Today technology allows us to look billions of light-years into outer space. Now, you tell me if there's a dragon with a tail long enough to sweep down all the stars of heaven some billions of light-years away. That's a pretty big dragon. This passage is talking about the devil. The stars are the fallen angels that fell. That is symbolism.

Let me give you an example from everyday life. When you're driving down the highway and you see the yellow arches, you know that you're approaching a McDonald's. When you see those yellow arches, do you say, "Oh, that's just a symbol. There is no McDonald's restaurant, and there is no such thing as a hamburger"? Of course not. The arches are a symbol of a reality.

You find out what the symbol stands for, and then you literally apply it.

When you get the Word of God, pray over it, ponder it, and then ask God to teach you. Here are six age-old questions to ask when studying the Word of God.

1. Is there a promise to claim?
2. Is there a lesson to learn?
3. Is there a blessing to enjoy?
4. Is there a command to obey?
5. Is there a sin to avoid?
6. Is there a new thought to carry with me?

These are great starter questions when preparing a Sunday school lesson or a Bible study. You can take any passage of Scripture and ask those questions and you've got your lesson! I promise you. Just ask these six simple questions as you study the Word of God, and God will give you the lesson He wants you to learn.

Preserve the Word of God

After you pray and ponder over the Word of God, then you preserve the Word of God. Psalm 119:11 says, "Your word I have hidden in my heart, that I might not sin against You." Verse 16 of that same psalm says, "I will delight myself in Your statutes; I will not forget Your word."

That means that you hide the Word of God in your heart. You can remember far more than you think you can remember. In fact, we function by memory. Memory comes with concentration, motivation, and use. Your mind is a marvel, and you can remember far more than you think you can remember as you preserve the Word of God.

My wife enjoys collecting pretty little boxes. Sometimes people will bring her boxes from other countries. They may be intricately carved or covered in jewels. You see one and say, "What a marvelous little box." Then you open it up to look inside. Do you know what's inside that beautiful little box? It contains things like rubber bands, paper clips, toothpicks, or an old breath mint. Your mind is like that box. God gave you a marvelous mind, and you've got all this junk in it.

Your mind can also be compared to a garden. Have you ever noticed how much easier it is to grow weeds than flowers and vegetables? When Adam fell, his mind became a garden of weeds. In order for your mind to preserve the Word of God, you have to cultivate your mind. You have to weed your garden. Fill your mind with the Word of God so what is inside will flow forth blessing and honor to God.

Practice the Word of God

Psalm 119:1–5 says, "Blessed are the undefiled in the way, who walk in the law of the LORD! Blessed are those who keep His testimonies, who seek Him with the whole heart! They also do no iniquity; they walk in His ways. You have commanded us to keep Your precepts diligently. Oh, that my ways were directed to keep Your statutes!"

It's not enough to *recite* the promises without *obeying* the commandments. Do you want to learn more about the Word of

God? Then obey the part you already know. That is so simple. The Bible says, "For whoever has, to him more will be given, and he will have abundance" (Matt. 13:12).

The more you obey, the more you will learn. You might be saying to yourself, "There's a lot of the Bible I don't understand." Do you know what Mark Twain is reported to have said? "It's not that part of the Bible I don't understand that gives me so much trouble. It's the part I do understand." Keep the Word of God!

There may be mysteries and things you don't understand like the third toe on the left foot of a beast in Revelation. But I will tell you one thing you *can* understand, "Love one another." You can understand when the Bible gives you clear and plain commandments. And, if you will begin to keep the things that you *do* understand, the Word of God will become real to you.

Proclaim the Word of God

Psalm 119:13 says, "With my lips I have declared all the judgments of Your mouth." Look at verse 27: "Make me understand the way of Your precepts; so shall I meditate on Your wonderful works." Then, in verse 46: "I will speak of Your testimonies also before kings, and will not be ashamed." Finally, look at verse 172: "My tongue shall speak of Your word, for all Your commandments are righteousness."

Let the Word of God be constantly in your mouth. Stow it in your heart, show it in your life, sow it in the world. The more of the Word of God you give away, the more of it will stick to you.

Appropriate the Values of the Word of God

You must *appreciate the virtues* of the Word of God, *assimilate the vitality* of the Word of God, *appropriate the values* of the Word of God. When you do that, this knowledge will transform your life.

A Source of Victory

Psalm 119:45 says, "And I will walk at liberty, for I seek Your precepts." Just as Jesus appropriated the Word of God to overcome Satan in the wilderness, so you can overcome. The Word of God can become your source of victory.

A Source of Growth

Psalm 119:32 says, "I will run the course of Your commandments, for You shall enlarge my heart."

A person might come to me and say, "I'm just so weak in my physical life. I can hardly get out of bed. I just don't want to go to work. I'm just so weak."

Then I might say, "What's the matter? Have you been to the doctor?"

"No," he says.

"Have you got a disease?"

"I don't think so," he says.

"What are you eating?"

"I have this restaurant I go to on Sundays sometimes if it's not raining, and I get a meal there. That's all I eat," he says.

"You mean that's all you eat? You just go to this restaurant on Sunday, and you get a meal there if it's not raining? And that's all you eat?"

"Yeah, I'm just so weak."

Well, of course he's weak.

Friend, a sermon on Sunday is designed just to whet your appetite. If you don't learn how to feed yourself the Word of God, you're not going to grow. The Bible says, "As newborn babes, desire the pure milk of the word, that you may grow thereby" (1 Pet. 2:2). The Word of God is your source of growth.

A Source of Joy

Psalm 119:54 says, "Your statutes have been my songs in the house of my pilgrimage."

Verse 111 of this psalm says, "Your testimonies I have taken as a heritage forever, for they are the rejoicing of my heart."

In John 15:11, Jesus said, "These things I have spoken to you, that My joy may remain in you, and that your joy may be full." The Word of God is a source of joy.

A Source of Power

The Word of God is your power source for victorious living. "For the word of God is living and powerful" (Heb. 4:12).

Psalm 119:28 says, "My soul melts from heaviness; strengthen me according to Your word." The Bible is our source of power.

A Source of Guidance

Psalm 119:105 says, "Your word is a lamp to my feet and a light to my path." We can find our way when we study and meditate upon His Word. It may be dark, but His Word will show us the way if we trust Him.

Do you want victory? Do you want growth? Do you want joy? Do you want power? Do you want guidance? Friend, the Word of God will give you all of these things. You can appropriate them. But you can only appropriate them after you assimilate them. And you can only assimilate them if you appreciate them. I promise you that if you'll do these things, the Word of God will transform your life.

STUDY QUESTIONS

1. How much time per day do you typically spend in the Word of God? How does that commitment compare with the amount of time you spend on other daily activities and habits? Do you feel like you allow yourself adequate time to understand and learn from it each day?

2. What books, chapters, or sections of the Bible do you find particularly engaging and enriching to you? What is it exactly about those portions of Scripture that speaks to you so profoundly and personally?

3. What other areas of the Bible do you typically avoid in your reading and study? How might you open yourself to exploring an

unfamiliar passage of Scripture, seeing how God could use it to speak to you in unexpected ways?

4. "Man shall not live by bread alone, but by every word that proceeds from the mouth of God" (Matt. 4:4). What if your desire for the Word was akin to those motivations that draw you to the breakfast, lunch, and dinner table—even to the pantry for in-between-meal snacks?

5. How does meditating on the Word of God differ from the more traditional, very mystical understanding of meditation that most people think of? How has mulling over a single Scripture verse throughout the day yielded new insights for you into what God is saying?

6. Paul said many of the stories and accounts from the Old Testament are meant to be "examples" to us (1 Cor. 10:6), ways to learn important spiritual lessons. Consider one or two events from the Old Testament, and ponder what you could apply from those?

7. What are some of the specific character traits God is growing and developing in you. (It's helpful to see areas of growth in ourselves, not just cause for discouragement.) How can you tie your desire for these qualities directly back to the Scripture for inspiration?

Epilogue

It's Not How Much You Know, It's How Much You *Grow*

"Knowledge puffs up, but love edifies" (1 Cor. 8:1).

I opened this book with the proposition that what you don't know *can* hurt you. Unfortunately, for some, knowledge and doctrine become an end in themselves.

The ultimate yardstick of your life as a believer is not how much you know but how much you *grow*. The purpose of this book has not been primarily information or inspiration but transformation.

Paul tells the aim of his ministry to the church at Ephesus.

". . . till we all come to the unity of the faith and of the knowledge of the Son of God, to a perfect man, to the measure of the stature of the fullness of Christ; that we should no longer be children, tossed to and fro and carried about with every wind of doctrine, by the trickery of men, in the cunning craftiness of deceitful plotting, but, speaking the truth in love, may grow up in all things into Him who

*is the head—Christ—from whom the whole body, joined
and knit together by what every joint supplies, according to
the effective working by which every part does its share,
causes growth of the body for the edifying of itself in love."
(Eph. 4:13–16)*

In this passage Paul was telling the saints to grow up.

We Are to Be Mature in Stature

*". . . till we all come to the unity of the faith and of the
knowledge of the Son of God, to a perfect man, to the
measure of the stature of the fullness of Christ." (Eph. 4:13)*

When I was a kid, my parents let us stand against a wall in the house. A mark was then placed on the wall that measured our height. From time to time, we would stand with our backs straight against that wall to see if we were growing. I remember stretching myself as tall as I could. Then my parents would measure my growth with the yardstick.

God measures His children with a different standard, "the measure of the stature of the fullness of Christ."

The standard and goal of your maturity is that you are to be like the Lord Jesus Christ. As a kid, I would measure my growth against that of my brother. It is time that we as Christians quit comparing ourselves with others and measure ourselves by Him. We may look fairly good if we compare ourselves with others, but Jesus is the standard. Are you becoming more and more like Him?

We Are to Be Mature in Stability

". . . that we should no longer be children, tossed to and fro and carried about with every wind of doctrine, by the trickery of men, in the cunning craftiness of deceitful plotting." (Eph. 4:14)

There are those who by cunning craftiness are ready to lead the immature Christian astray. It is heartbreaking to see many immature Christians who are led into false cults and bizarre beliefs. I used to be amazed that some would not believe. After many years, I am now even more amazed at what some will believe.

G. K. Chesterton is reported to have said, "When men stop believing in God, it is not that they then believe in nothing. Rather, it is that they will believe in anything." I might add that if Christians are not firmly rooted and growing, they too are apt to believe almost anything. They are "sitting ducks" for Satan's big guns.

The average pastor is heartsick over immature Christians who are lost, strayed, or stolen. Genuine truth ought to help you to be a steadfast Christian.

We Are to be Mature in Speech

". . . but, speaking the truth in love, may grow up in all things into Him who is the head—Christ." (Eph. 4:15)

Why are there so many in the church with hurt feelings? And why is there so much division in modern Christianity? One of the chief reasons is immature Christians who act like children in their speech. Of course, we must speak the truth. That is a given. That's why we have written *What Every Christian Ought to Know*. But we need more than Bible truth. We need love that comes with Christian growth and maturity.

There need be no division between truth and love. Some have made that division. Truth without love may be a form of brutality. Love without truth may be empty sentimentality. May God deliver us from the immature pronouncements of those who have loveless truth and the immature emotionalism of those who have truthless love.

With truth and no love one may swell up. With love and no truth one may blow up. But truth and love cause the Christian to grow up.

We Are to Be Mature in Service

". . . from whom the whole body, joined and knit together by what every joint supplies, according to the effective working by which every part does its share, causes growth of the body for the edifying of itself in love." (Eph. 4:16)

Each part in a healthy body helps the other parts, each in its own way. By love we serve one another.

This verse speaks of the church as a body and mentions joints. The Greek word for joint is *harmos*. We get our word *harmony* from this word. Mature people work together in harmonious interaction like the joints in a body. Mature people can work together if the joints of the body (the church) are lubricated with love. This comes with maturity.

A cathedral in England was destroyed by German bombs during World War II. Some students helped to rebuild it. A statue of Jesus in the cathedral had been damaged. The students pieced it together, but the hands had been destroyed beyond retrieval. Rather than replace the hands, they placed a plaque beneath the statue that read, "Christ has no hands but ours." There is a great truth to that. May God help you to find a place of service and let your hands be His hands.

As we bring all of this to a conclusion, remember that you are to grow with what you have learned. Keep growing! Remember that when you cease to be better, you will cease to be good.

Notes

Chapter 1, "Every Christian Ought to Know the Bible Is the Word of God"

1. W. A. Criswell, *The Bible for Today's World* (Grand Rapids: Zondervan, 1965), 17.

2. Ibid., 17.

3. William Wilson gives these meanings for the Hebrew *chuwg*: "circle, sphere, the arch or vault of the heavens; the circle of the earth, *orbis terrarium.*" William Wilson, *New Wilson's Old Testament Word Studies* (Grand Rapids: Kregel, 1987).

4. S. I. McMillen, *None of These Diseases* (Grand Rapids: Fleming H. Revell Co., 2001).

Chapter 2, "Every Christian Ought to Know the Assurance of Salvation"

1. "That He might sanctify and cleanse her with the washing of water by the word" (Eph. 5:26). "Having been born again, not of corruptible seed but incorruptible, through the word of God which lives and abides forever" (1 Pet. 1:23).

STEPS TO PEACE WITH GOD

1. GOD'S PURPOSE: PEACE AND LIFE

God loves you and wants you to experience peace and life—abundant and eternal.

THE BIBLE SAYS ...

"We have peace with God through our Lord Jesus Christ." *Romans 5:1, NIV*

"For God so loved the world that He gave His only begotten Son, that whoever believes in Him should not perish but have everlasting life." *John 3:16, NKJV*

"I have come that they may have life, and that they may have it more abundantly." *John 10:10, NKJV*

Since God planned for us to have peace and the abundant life right now, why are most people not having this experience?

2. OUR PROBLEM: SEPARATION FROM GOD

God created us in His own image to have an abundant life. He did not make us as robots to automatically love and obey Him, but gave us a will and a freedom of choice.

We chose to disobey God and go our own willful way. We still make this choice today. This results in separation from God.

THE BIBLE SAYS ...

"For all have sinned and fall short of the glory of God." *Romans 3:23, NIV*

"For the wages of sin is death, but the gift of God is eternal life in Christ Jesus our Lord." *Romans 6:23, NIV*

Our choice results in separation from God.

OUR ATTEMPTS

Through the ages, individuals have tried in many ways to bridge this gap ... without success ...

THE BIBLE SAYS ...

"There is a way that appears to be right, but in the end it leads to death."
Proverbs 14:12, NIV

"But your iniquities have separated you from your God; and your sins have hidden His face from you, so that He will not hear."
Isaiah 59:2, NKJV

There is only one remedy for this problem of separation.

3. GOD'S REMEDY: THE CROSS

Jesus Christ is the only answer to this problem. He died on the cross and rose from the grave, paying the penalty for our sin and bridging the gap between God and people.

THE BIBLE SAYS ...

"For there is one God and one mediator between God and mankind, the man Christ Jesus."
1 Timothy 2:5, NIV

"For Christ also suffered once for sins, the just for the unjust, that He might bring us to God."
1 Peter 3:18, NKJV

"But God demonstrates His own love toward us, in that while we were still sinners, Christ died for us." *Romans 5:8, NKJV*

God has provided the only way ... we must make the choice ...

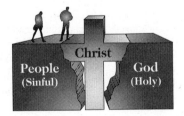

4. OUR RESPONSE: RECEIVE CHRIST

We must trust Jesus Christ and receive Him by personal invitation.

THE BIBLE SAYS ...

"Behold, I stand at the door and knock. If anyone hears My voice and opens the door, I will come in to him and dine with him, and he with Me." *Revelation 3:20, NKJV*

"But as many as received Him, to them He gave the right to become children of God, to those who believe in His name." *John 1:12, NKJV*

"If you confess with your mouth the Lord Jesus and believe in your heart that God has raised Him from the dead, you will be saved." *Romans 10:9, NKJV*

Are you here ... or here?

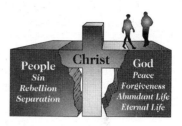

Is there any good reason why you cannot receive Jesus Christ right now?

HOW TO RECEIVE CHRIST:

1. Admit your need (say, "I am a sinner").
2. Be willing to turn from your sins (repent) and ask for God's forgiveness.
3. Believe that Jesus Christ died for you on the cross and rose from the grave.
4. Through prayer, invite Jesus Christ to come in and control your life through the Holy Spirit (receive Jesus as Lord and Savior).

WHAT TO PRAY:

Dear Lord Jesus,
    I know that I am a sinner, and I ask for Your forgiveness. I believe You died for my sins and rose from the dead. I turn from my sins and invite You to come into my heart and life. I want to trust and follow You as my Lord and Savior.

In Your Name, amen.

_____   _____
Date   Signature

IF YOU PRAYED THIS PRAYER,

THE BIBLE SAYS ...

"For, 'Everyone who calls on the name of the Lord will be saved.'"
Romans 10:13, NIV

Did you sincerely ask Jesus Christ to come into your life?
Where is He right now? What has He given you?

"For it is by grace you have been saved, through faith—and this not from
yourselves, it is the gift of God—not by works, so that no one can boast."
Ephesians 2:8–9, NIV

THE BIBLE SAYS ...

"He who has the Son has life; he who does not have the Son of God does
not have life. These things I have written to you who believe in the name of
the Son of God, that you may know that you have eternal life, and that you
may continue to believe in the name of the Son of God."
1 John 5:12–13, NKJV

Receiving Christ, we are born into God's family through the
supernatural work of the Holy Spirit who indwells every believer.
This is called regeneration or the "new birth."

This is just the beginning of a wonderful new life in Christ. To deepen
this relationship you should:

1. Read your Bible every day to know Christ better.
2. Talk to God in prayer every day.
3. Tell others about Christ.
4. Worship, fellowship, and serve with other Christians in a church where Christ
   is preached.
5. As Christ's representative in a needy world, demonstrate your new life by
   your love and concern for others.

God bless you as you do.

Billy Graham

If you want further help in the decision you have made, write to:
Billy Graham Evangelistic Association
1 Billy Graham Parkway, Charlotte, NC 28201-0001

1-877-2GRAHAM (1-877-247-2426)
BillyGraham.org/Commitment

LET YOUR FAITH TAKE ROOT

Whether you are just beginning your faith journey or have been a believer for decades, *What Every Christian Ought to Know* will establish you in the core truths of the Bible, equip you to confidently articulate your faith, and empower you to live a dynamic Christian life. In his refreshingly relatable style, Dr. Rogers covers essential topics such as **salvation, eternal security, prayer, the Holy Spirit, resisting temptation,** and **finding God's will** and unpacks their practical application for your everyday Christian walk.

One of Adrian Rogers' most popular books, this new edition includes an introduction from Steve Rogers, president of the Adrian Rogers Pastor Training Institute, plus discussion questions for personal reflection or group study.

"There is no one in America whom I respected more."
—JAMES DOBSON

"Adrian Rogers was a true spiritual giant."
—BEVERLY LAHAYE

"We need ministers to defend the Bible as the infallible Word of God. I believe in my heart Adrian Rogers was such a man."
—BILLY GR

ADRIAN ROGERS was one of America's most respected Bible teachers, communicating to millions through his *Love Worth Finding* radio and television ministry which continues today. He was also senior pastor of the 27,000-member Bellevue Baptist Church near Memphis, Tennessee, and a popular author whose books include *Unveiling the End Times in Our Time* and *The Incredible Power of Kingdom Authority.*

STEVE ROGERS is president of the Adrian Rogers Pastor Training Institute.

A *Billy Graham Library Selection* designates materials that are appropriate for a well-rounded collection of quality Christian literature, including both classic and contemporary reading and reference materials.

BILLY GRAHAM
Evangelistic Association
Always Good News.

ISBN 978-1-59328-395-7

00000

9 781593 283957

1-877-2GRAHAM (1-877-247-2426)
BillyGraham.org

5401t